Horst Hamann

for Hendrik and Peter

London Vertical

Horst Hamann

teNeues

"I have often called London an analogue city rather than a digital one such as New York. The structure of the city, with its absence of grids and numerical references, is more organic, having evolved out of individual centres that have developed and coalesced over time. Each place has its own green space or, occasionally in the metropolitan centre, its own urban space, such as a square, to define it."

5

"I have often called London an analogue city rather than a digital one such as New York. The structure of the city, with its absence of grids and numerical references, is more organic, having evolved out of individual centres that have developed and coalesced over time. Each place has its own green space or, occasionally in the metropolitan centre, its own urban space, such as a square, to define it."

Content

Michael Hoppen 8

When someone falls in love with London we should pay attention. Our wonderful grimy and bustling city is the focus of this new remarkable book by Horst Hamann, "London Vertical".

I have known Horst for many years and when he came to me with an idea of vertical panoramas of London my interest was immediately piqued. London is one of the most underphotographed cities in the west. Why do Paris and New York find themselves under the gaze of so many famous photographs through the ages? What is it that makes London so hard to photograph – Is she not photogenic? Do her mixed architectural styles make her the ugly duckling of Europe? I think not. I think it just needed the right photographer, in this case Horst Hamann, to find the right medium and right moment to cast his eye over our grand city. A vertical panoramic image is not one we see often as it disrupts the normal "eye-view".

The resulting photographs show a different London to the one we imagine. Stretched by virtue of his chosen panoramic format, London becomes a serene and quite beautiful 21st century urban jewel. Her history and complexity are now all clearly displayed for us to see and reflect on. Great cities are made up of many cultural layers and London is no exception: from its centre to inside its myriad of wonderful buildings.

With his long awaited new book, Horst Hamann invites us to reassess the city we thought we knew and provides us, the viewer, with a new and beautifully crafted version to enjoy.

Wenn sich jemand in die Stadt London verliebt, sollte man aufhorchen. Unsere wunderbar schmuddelige und lebendige Stadt steht im Mittelpunkt dieses neuen bemerkenswerten Buches von Horst Hamann, „London Vertical".

Ich kenne Horst seit vielen Jahren und als er mit der Idee zu mir kam, vertikale Panoramaaufnahmen von London machen zu wollen, war ich sofort Feuer und Flamme. London gehört zu den am wenigsten fotografierten westlichen Städten. Warum wurden Paris und New York in all den Jahren von so vielen berühmten Fotografen vor die „Linse" genommen? Weshalb lässt sich London so schwer fotografieren – ist die Stadt nicht fotogen? Ist sie aufgrund ihrer gemischten architektonischen Baustile das hässliche Entlein Europas? Ich glaube nicht. Vielmehr denke ich, es musste einfach der richtige Fotograf kommen, in diesem Fall Horst Hamann, um das richtige Medium und den richtigen Moment zu finden für einen neuen Blick auf unsere große Stadt. Ein vertikales Panoramabild sehen wir nicht oft; es stört die normale Perspektive.

Die entstandenen Fotos zeigen ein ganz anderes, neues London. Gestreckt durch das gewählte Panoramaformat wird London zu einer ruhigen und einfach schönen urbanen Perle des 21. Jahrhunderts. Die Geschichte und Komplexität der Stadt sind nun für uns alle deutlich sichtbar und nachvollziehbar. Großstädte bestehen aus vielen Kulturschichten und London bildet da keine Ausnahme: Von seiner Mitte bis ins Herz der vielfältigen, wunderschönen Gebäude.

Mit dem lang ersehnten neuen Buch lädt Horst Hamann uns ein, die Stadt, die wir zu kennen glaubten, neu zu entdecken. Er bietet uns, dem Betrachter, eine neue, ungewöhnliche Sicht auf London an.

9

Roger Ridsdill Smith   Head of Structural Engineering
                              Foster + Partners

Some words sit naturally beside one another, their combined meaning clearly understood and unquestioned – right angle, ice cream, United Kingdom. By the same token, it seemed like a natural move when Horst Hamann put 'vertical' and 'New York' together for his extraordinary collection of photographs of the city. No further explanation was required. The phrase felt like a poster campaign, or the top predictive text for an internet search. Combining 'vertical' and 'London', though, is more of a challenge, a provocation that requires further thought.

London has always had an ambiguous relationship with height. The architectural debates surrounding high-rise structures towards the end of the century evoked two broad lines of questioning. Firstly, were tower blocks the solution to the dense and generally low-quality brick terraced housing built during and after the Industrial Revolution, or were they a new form of social inequality, fragmenting communities and creating isolated monotenure estates within the city? The latter position might be the more widely held view today, however there was an idealism behind the construction of these towers that is easily forgotten.

Secondly, what was the effect of tall buildings on the city's skyline, and in particular on the protected views of St Paul's Cathedral? At 111 metres, Christopher Wren's dome was the tallest structure in London, and it remained so from its completion in 1710 until 1967. Its silhouette is viewed from specific locations around the city to appraise the visual implications of new buildings. Would the construction of more towers permanently rob the city of its uniqueness?

With the beginning of the new Millennium, the focus shifted from these two questions. The debate instead addressed the ownership and use of new towers. Following the rush to build luxury residential developments in the centre of the city, was anyone actually living in these new buildings, or were they simply tax-efficient and secure investment vehicles? If at first sight this position appears cogent, its relevance to the general housing debate in the UK is questionable. The fact that a small percentage of the population can afford to buy properties that they do not always occupy should not divert attention from the need to build more homes for everyone else across the rest of the country.

Recently, the debate has focused on whether it is morally defensible to construct tall buildings at all in the current climate crisis, given that their construction uses more resources and, consequently, has a greater environmental impact than building at lower heights. This debate is in its early stages but current research from urban economists indicates, anti-intuitively perhaps, that the environmental footprint of living in low-density suburbs is greater than that of living in high-density city centres, a result principally of the greater reliance on carbon-intensive private car use in the suburbs.

In New York, towers are called skyscrapers. They are identified by their address, or by their occupier or, occasionally, by their financer. In London, our best-known high-rise landmarks are referred to by their shape and, in particular, by a formal similarity to another object. Is this affectionate or pejorative? Maybe by calling them nicknames, we neutralise the impact of these buildings on the city without any further need to consider each of them individually on their architectural merits.

So how does Hamann resolve the dilemma of using the same descriptor for two cities, London and New York, with such profoundly different attitudes to verticality? The answer is by reversing the proposition. Instead of referring to the building, he refers to the photograph. Rather than the subject dictating the format, the format dictates the subject. Hamann's photographs of London are juxtapositions. Images are carved out in strong crisp lines – the structure of a roof, the edge of a building facade, or the corners of a sculpture. Many of the compositions could be redrawn using a thick black brushstroke in a single unbroken line, like a piece of calligraphy. The long vertical format, a subconscious shock to the normal 4 × 3 landscape format we are used to, forces us to focus on the deliberateness of the image. These shots are not a view of the city. They are cut out of a view of the city, a rectangular keyhole, and printed in strong contrast against a silver white sky.

Buildings that have reached the status of postcard fodder, seen so many times that they have lost all meaning, are suddenly viewed from a different perspective. The results are surprising. 30 St Mary Axe (The Gherkin) appears to be almost touching its neighbour. The Lodon Eye hovers over Big Ben like a spaceship. Sir Anthony Caro's sculpture announcing the Millennium Bridge at Queen Victoria Street towers above St Paul's dome – an irony bearing in mind that one of the features of the shallow bridge structure was that it managed to slot above the busy Thames navigation channel, while staying below the protected view of the cathedral.

Hamann's photos capture a specific moment in London's history, where the country has left Europe despite the majority of Londoners wishing to stay. Which way does the city evolve from this point? Does a gentle decline set in, and the mobile international community that has put down its roots here melt away? Or does London's serendipitous mix of commerce (finance, media, business) and chance (time zone, language) combine with the fact that it is, after all, a fantastic place to live, to provide enough momentum to carry the city through the current period of national reflection?

Time will tell. And when it does, Hamann will hopefully come back and interpret what it says.

Roger Ridsdill Smith   **Head of Structural Engineering
Foster + Partners**

Es gibt Wörter, die ganz natürlich nebeneinan-
derstehen, deren kombinierte Bedeutung
klar verstanden und nicht in Frage gestellt wird
– rechter Winkel, Eiscreme, Vereinigtes König-
reich. Aus demselben Grund erschien es als ein
natürlicher Schritt, als Horst Hamann „vertikal" und „New York" für seine außergewöhnli-
che Sammlung von Fotografien der Stadt
zusammenfügte. Eine weitere Erklärung war
nicht erforderlich. Der Satz wirkte wie eine
Plakatkampagne oder der erste Suchbegriff
bei einer Internetsuche. Die Kombination
von „vertikal" und „London" stellt jedoch eher
eine Herausforderung dar, eine Provokation,
die weitere Überlegungen erfordert.

London hatte schon immer ein zwiespältiges
Verhältnis zur Höhe. Die architektonischen
Debatten um Hochhäuser gegen Ende des Jahrhunderts riefen zwei große Fragestellungen
hervor. Erstens: Waren Hochhäuser die Lösung
für die dichten und im Allgemeinen minder-
wertigen Backsteinreihenhäuser, die während
und nach der industriellen Revolution gebaut
wurden, oder waren sie eine neue Form der sozialen Ungleichheit, die die Gemeinschaften
zersplitterte und isolierte Monopolsiedlungen
in der Stadt schuf? Die letztere Ansicht mag
heute weiterverbreitet sein, doch hinter dem
Bau dieser Türme stand ein Idealismus, der
leicht in Vergessenheit gerät.

Zweitens: Wie wirkten sich die hohen Gebäude
auf die Skyline der Stadt und insbesondere
auf die geschützte Aussicht auf die St Paul's Cà-
thedral aus? Mit 111 Metern war deren Kuppel
von Christopher Wren das höchste Bauwerk
Londons, und das blieb sie auch von ihrer
Fertigstellung im Jahr 1710 bis 1967. Deren Silhouette dient von bestimmten Standorten in
der Stadt aus betrachtet, der Beurteilung visu-
eller Auswirkungen neuer Gebäude. Würde
der Bau weiterer Türme die Stadt dauerhaft ihrer Einzigartigkeit berauben?

Mit dem Beginn des neuen Jahrtausends ver-
schob sich der Schwerpunkt von diesen beiden Fragen. Die Debatte drehte sich stattdes-
sen um die Eigentumsverhältnisse und die
Nutzung der neuen Hochhäuser. Würde nach
dem Ansturm auf den Bau von Luxuswohnun-
gen im Stadtzentrum überhaupt noch jemand
in diesen neuen Gebäuden wohnen, oder han-
delte es sich lediglich um steuereffiziente und
sichere Anlageformen? Auch wenn dieser
Standpunkt auf den ersten Blick schlüssig erscheint, ist seine Relevanz für die allgemeine
Wohnungsbaudiskussion im Vereinigten Köni-
reich fraglich. Die Tatsache, dass ein kleiner
Prozentsatz der Bevölkerung es sich leisten
kann, Immobilien zu kaufen, die er nicht immer selbst bewohnt, sollte nicht von der Notwen-
digkeit ablenken, im restlichen Land mehr
Wohnungen für alle anderen zu bauen.

In jüngster Zeit hat sich die Debatte auf die Frage konzentriert, ob es moralisch vertretbar
ist, in der gegenwärtigen Klimakrise überhaupt
hohe Gebäude zu bauen, da ihr Bau mehr
Ressourcen verbraucht und folglich größere
Auswirkungen auf die Umwelt hat als der Bau
von Gebäuden mit geringerer Höhe. Diese Debatte steckt noch in den Kinderschuhen, aber
aktuelle Forschungsergebnisse von Stadtöko-
nomen deuten darauf hin, dass der ökologi-
sche Fußabdruck in Vorstädten mit geringer
Bevölkerungsdichte größer ist als der in Stadt-
zentren mit hoher Bevölkerungsdichte, was
vor allem darauf zurückzuführen ist, dass in den
Vorstädten mehr private Autos eingesetzt
werden.

In New York werden die Hochhäuser Wolkenkratzer genannt. Sie werden nach ihrer Adresse,
ihrem Nutzer oder gelegentlich auch nach ihrem
Geldgeber benannt. In London werden unsere
bekanntesten Hochhäuser nach ihrer Form und
vor allem nach ihrer formalen Ähnlichkeit mit
einem anderen Objekt benannt. Ist dies liebevoll
oder abwertend? Vielleicht neutralisieren
wir die Wirkung dieser Gebäude auf die Stadt, indem wir ihnen Spitznamen geben, ohne dass
wir sie einzeln auf ihre architektonischen Vorzü-
ge hin untersuchen müssen.

Wie also löst Hamann das Dilemma, dass er für
zwei Städte, London und New York, mit so
unterschiedlichen Einstellungen zur Vertikalität
denselben Begriff verwendet? Die Antwort
liegt in der Umkehrung des Satzes. Anstatt sich
auf das Gebäude zu beziehen, bezieht er sich
auf die Fotografie. Nicht das Motiv diktiert das
Format, sondern das Format diktiert das Motiv.
Hamanns Fotografien von London sind Ne-
beneinanderstellungen. Die Bilder sind in star-
ken, klaren Linien gezeichnet – die Struktur
eines Daches, die Kante einer Gebäudefassade
oder die Ecken einer Skulptur. Viele der Kom-
positionen könnten mit einem dicken schwar-
zen Pinselstrich in einer einzigen ununterbro-
chenen Linie neu gezeichnet werden, wie eine
Kalligraphie. Das lange Hochformat, ein un-
bewusster Schock gegenüber dem normalen
4 × 3 Querformat, an das wir gewöhnt sind,
zwingt uns, uns auf die Bewusstheit des Bildes
zu konzentrieren. Diese Aufnahmen sind kein
Blick auf die Stadt. Sie sind aus einer Stadtan-
sicht, einem rechteckigen Schlüsselloch, aus-
geschnitten und in starkem Kontrast vor einem
silberweißen Himmel gedruckt.

Gebäude, die schon so oft gesehen wurden,
dass sie jede Bedeutung verloren haben, werden plötzlich aus einer anderen Perspektive
betrachtet. Die Ergebnisse sind überraschend.
30 St Mary Axe (The Gherkin) scheint seinen
Nachbarn fast zu berühren. Das London Eye
schwebt wie ein Raumschiff über Big Ben. Sir
Anthony Caros Skulptur, die die Millennium
Bridge in der Queen Victoria Street ankündigt,
überragt die Kuppel von St Paul's – eine Ironie,
wenn man bedenkt, dass eines der Merkmale
der flachen Brückenkonstruktion darin bestand, dass sie sich über dem viel befahrenen
Themse-Schifffahrtskanal befand, während
sie unter dem denkmalgeschützten Blick auf
die Kathedrale blieb.

Hamanns Fotos halten einen besonderen Moment in der Geschichte Londons fest, in dem
das Land Europa verlassen hat, obwohl die Mehr-
heit der Londoner gerne geblieben wäre. In
welche Richtung entwickelt sich die Stadt von
diesem Zeitpunkt an? Setzt ein sanfter Nie-
dergang ein, und die mobile internationale Ge-
meinschaft, die hier ihre Wurzeln geschlagen
hat, schmilzt dahin? Oder wird London glück-
liche Mischung aus Kommerz (Finanzen, Me-
dien, Wirtschaft) und Zufall (Zeitzone, Sprache)
in Verbindung mit der Tatsache, dass London
ein fantastischer Ort zum Leben ist, genug
Schwung liefern, um die Stadt durch die derzei-
tige Phase der nationalen Reflexion zu tragen?

Die Zeit wird es zeigen. Und wenn es soweit ist,
wird Hamann hoffentlich zurückkommen und
interpretieren, was sie sagt.

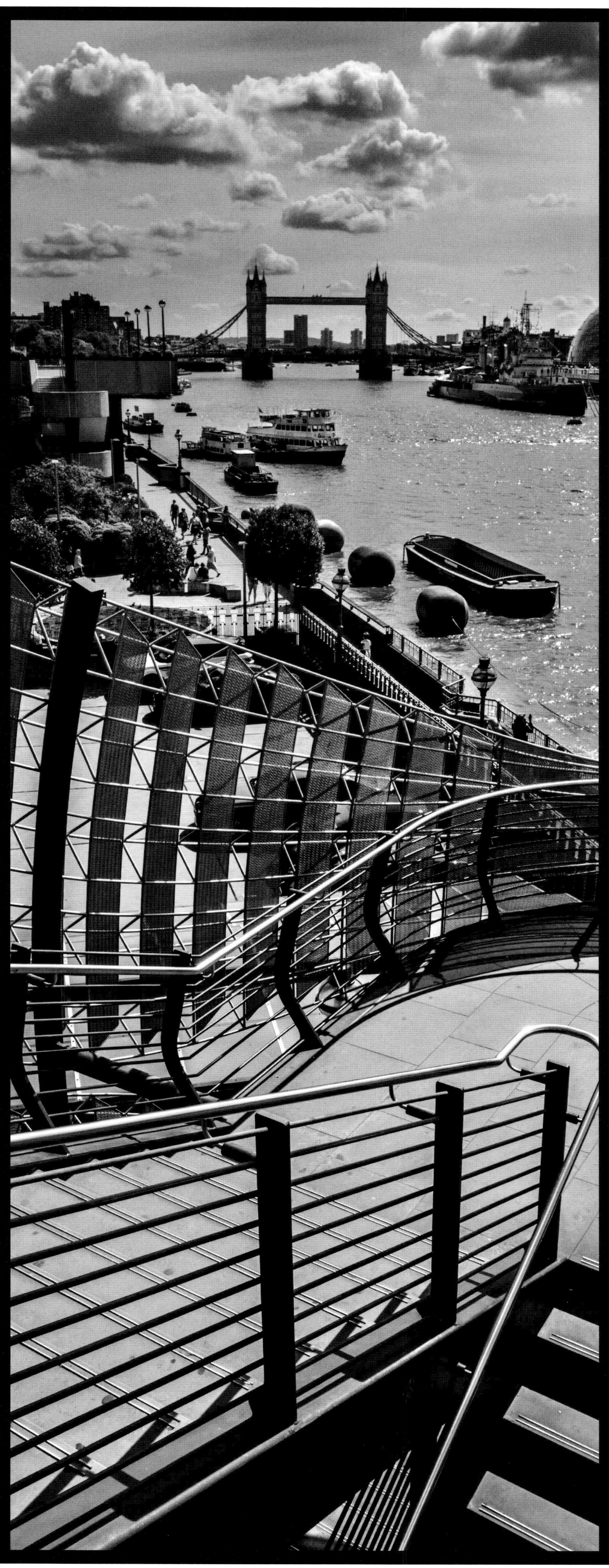

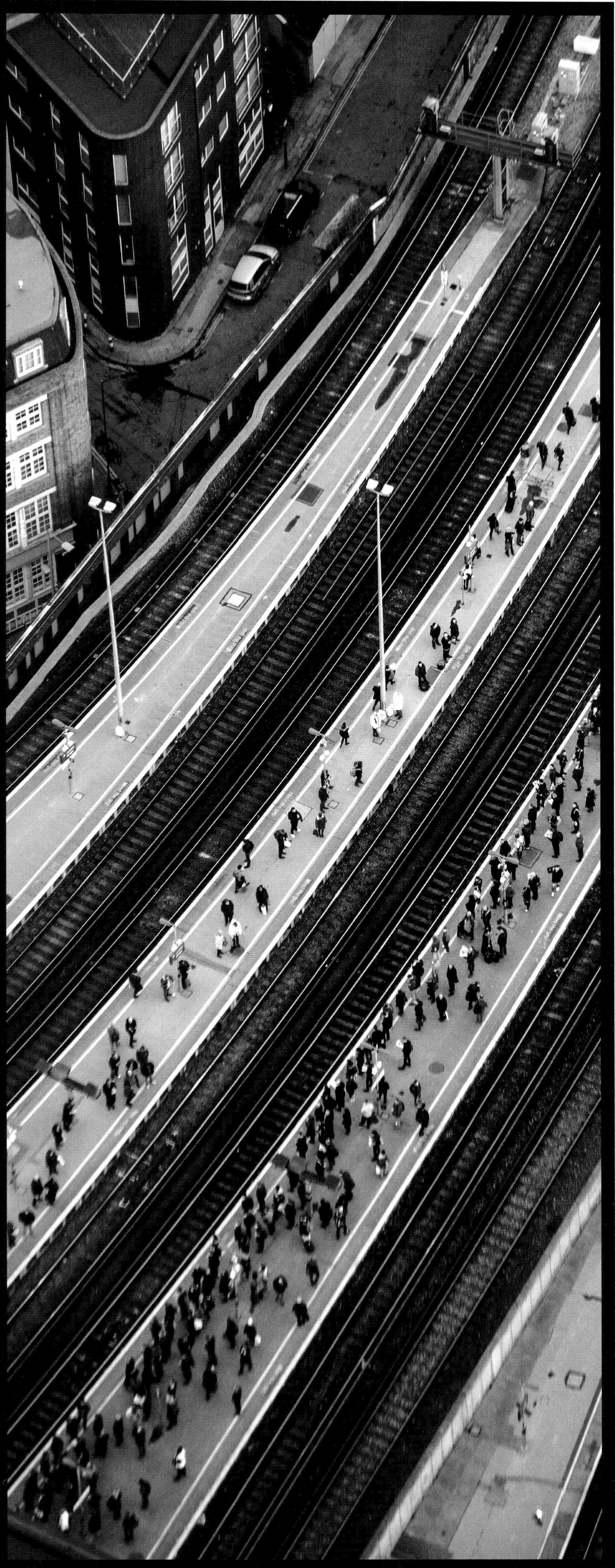

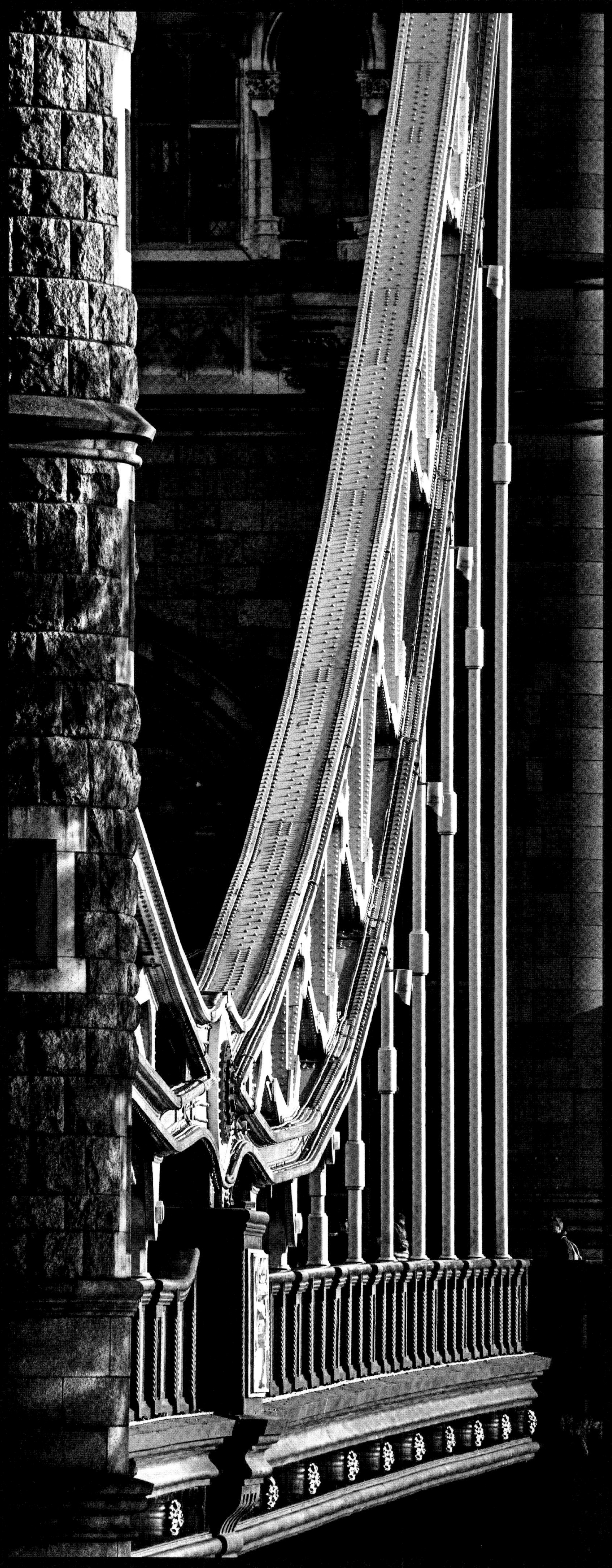

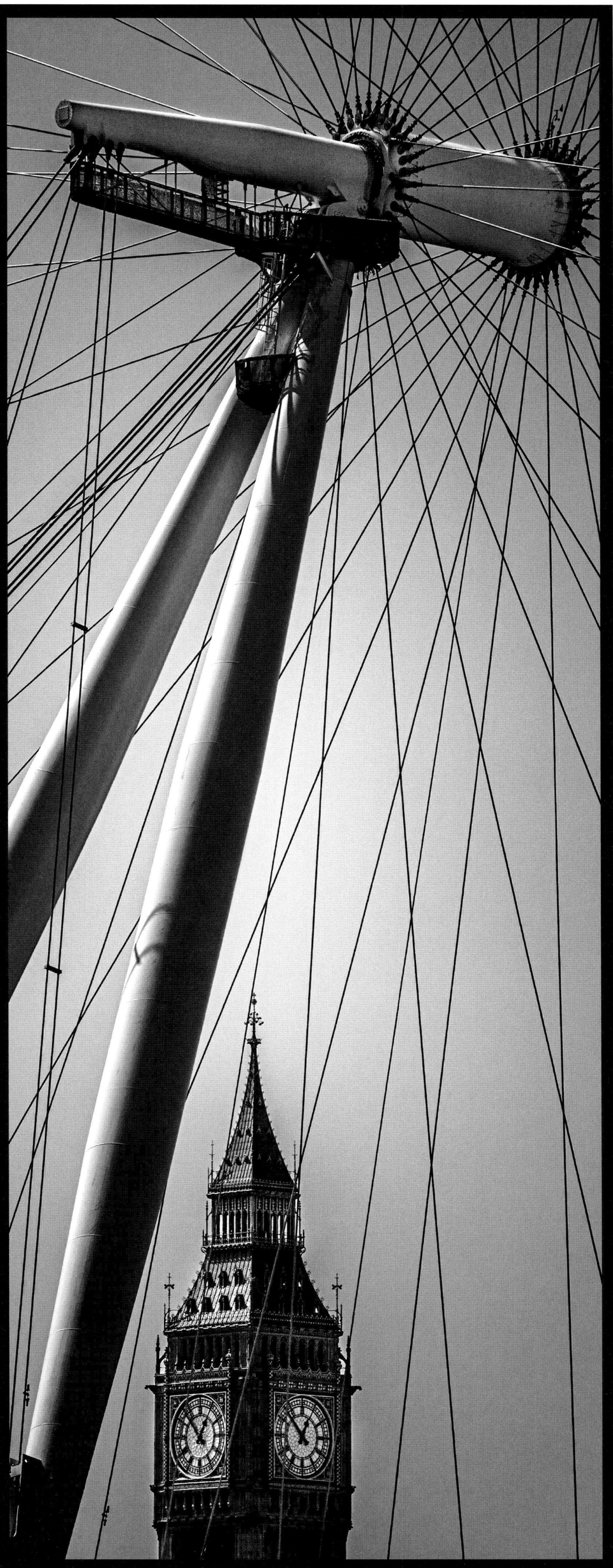

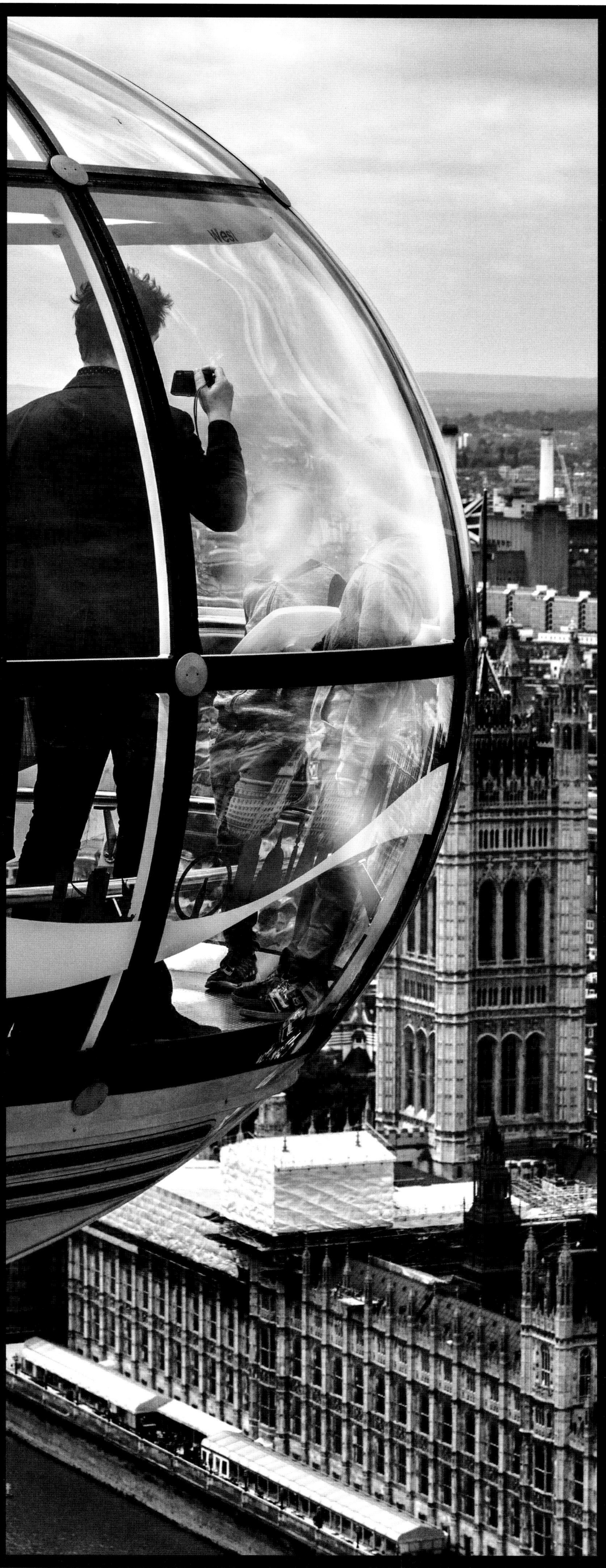
West

Vauxhall Bridge Statue / St Paul's Cathedral Miniature   24

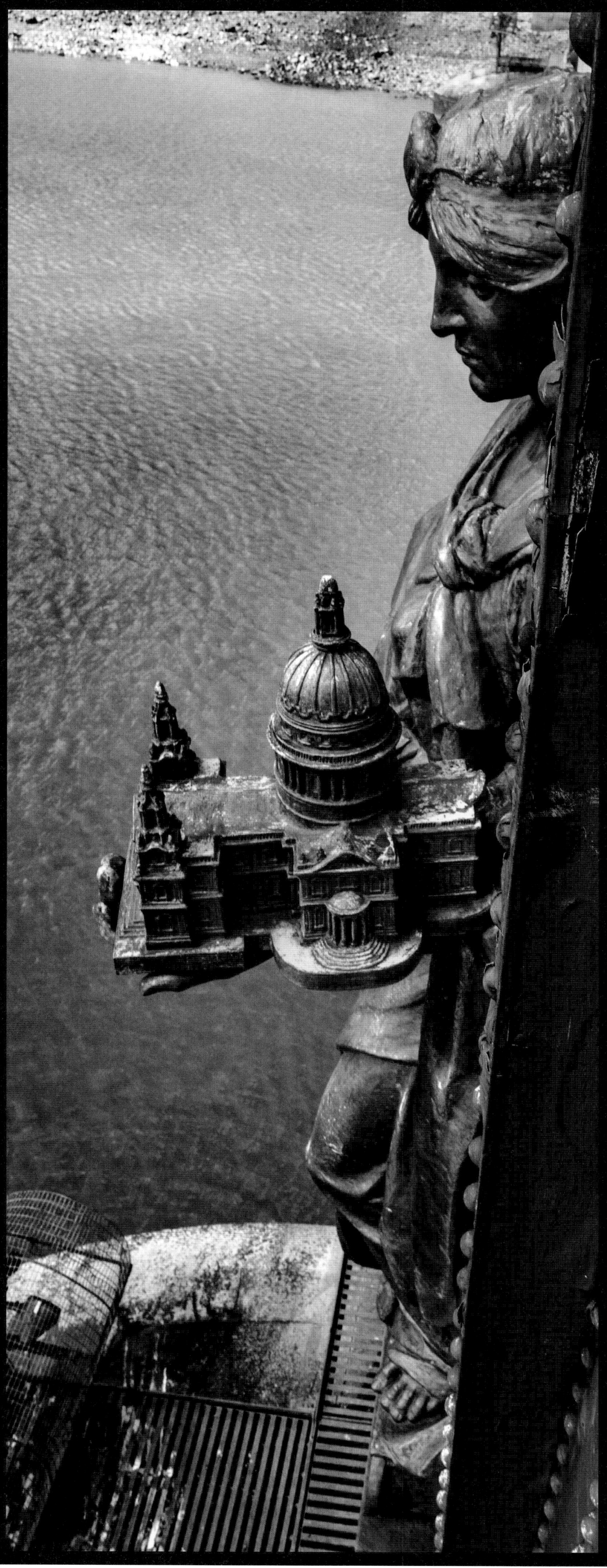

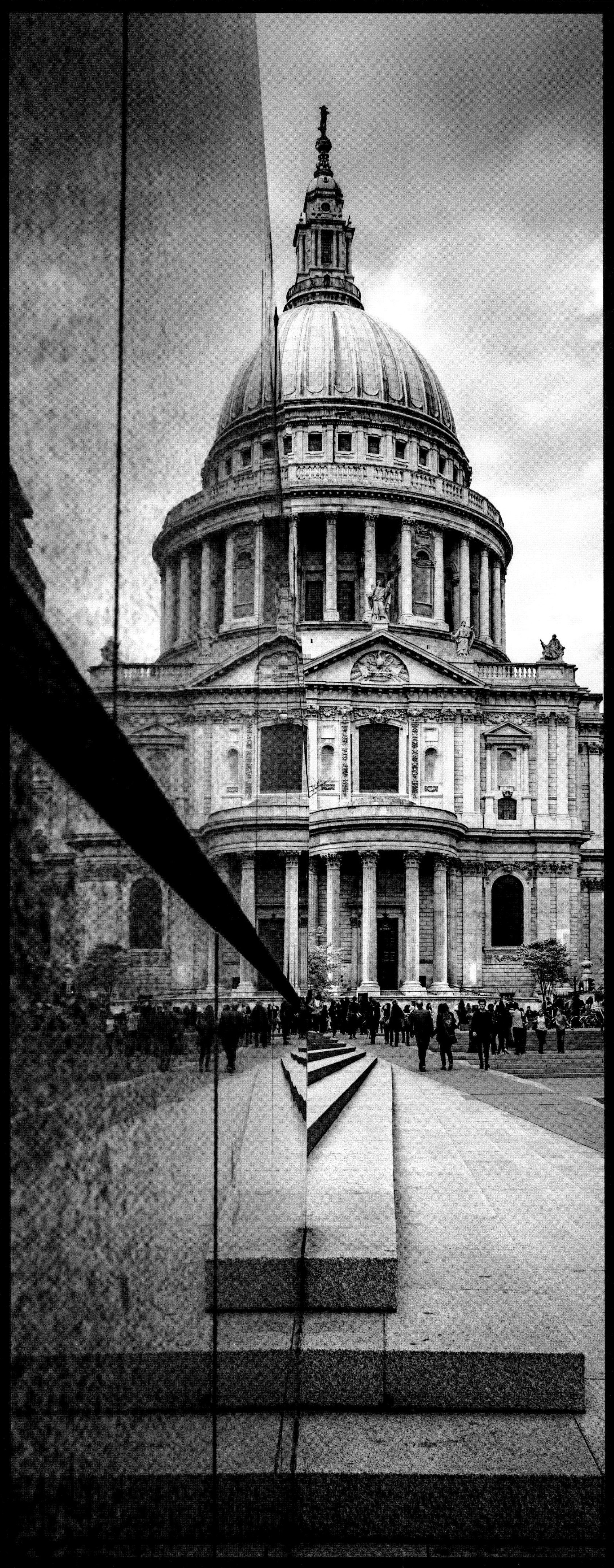

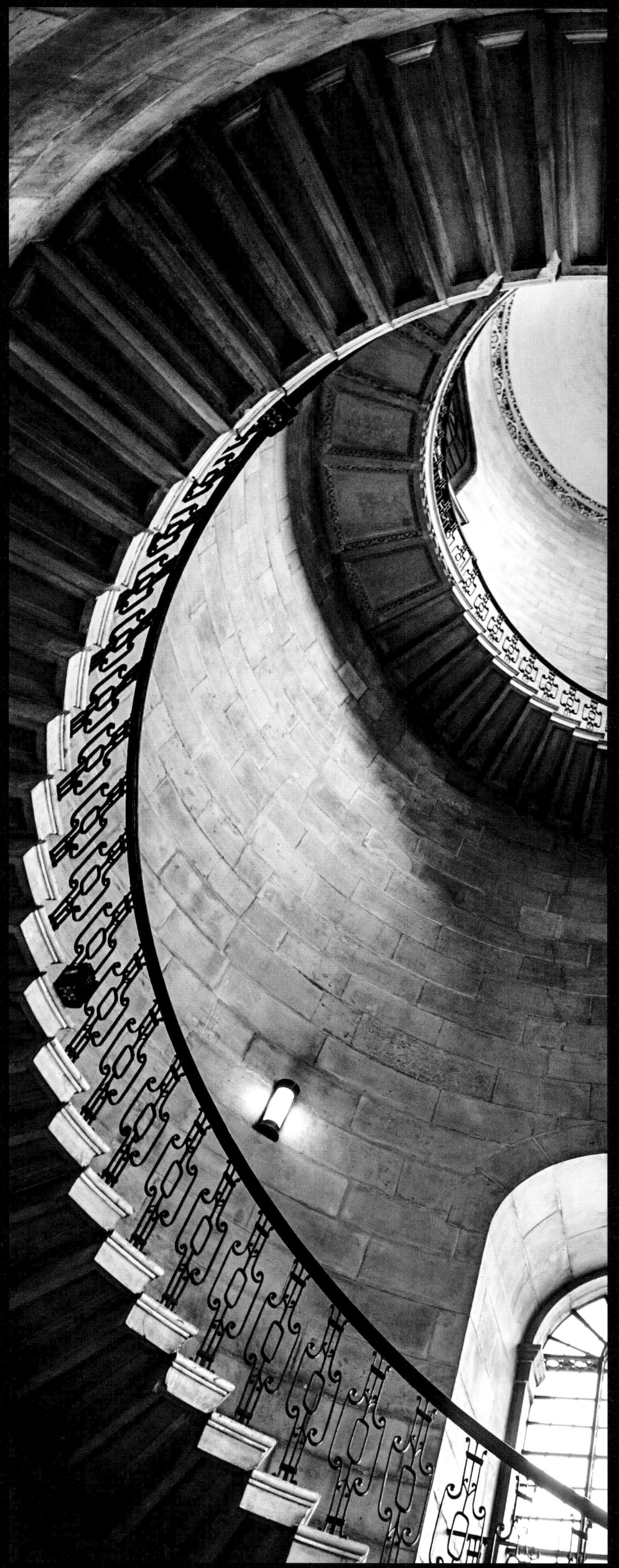

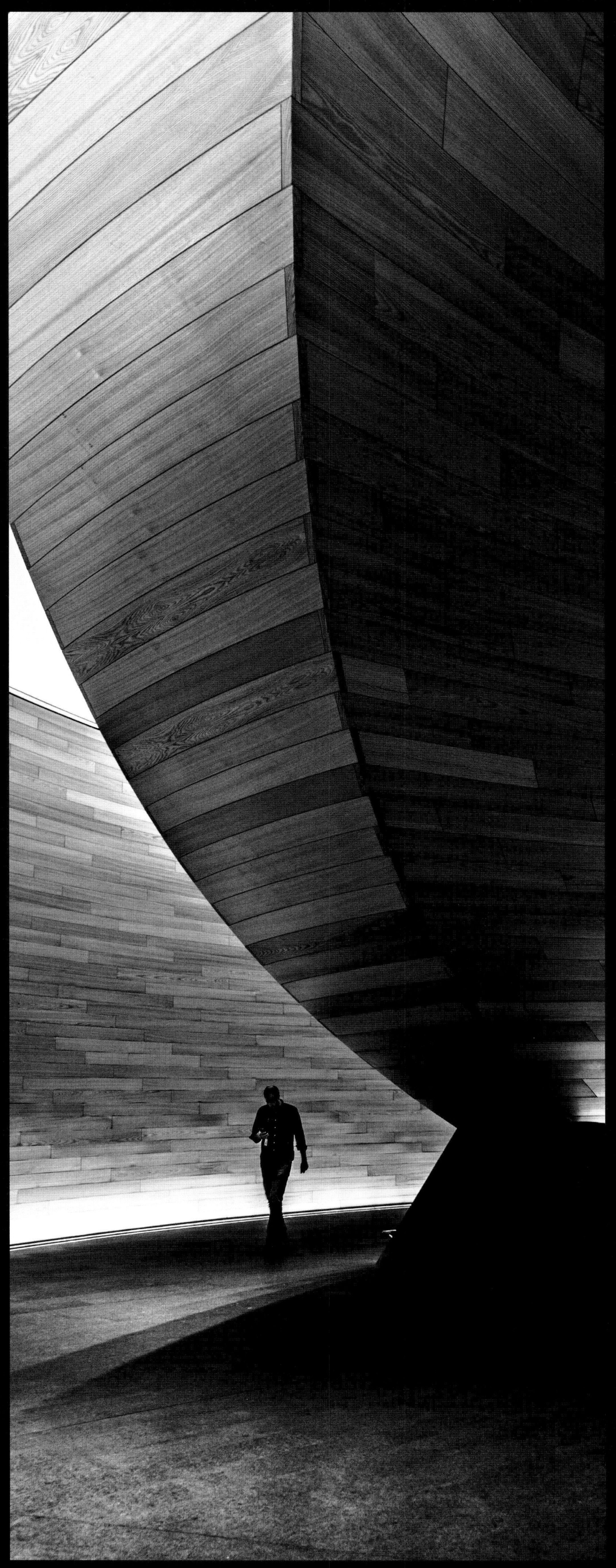

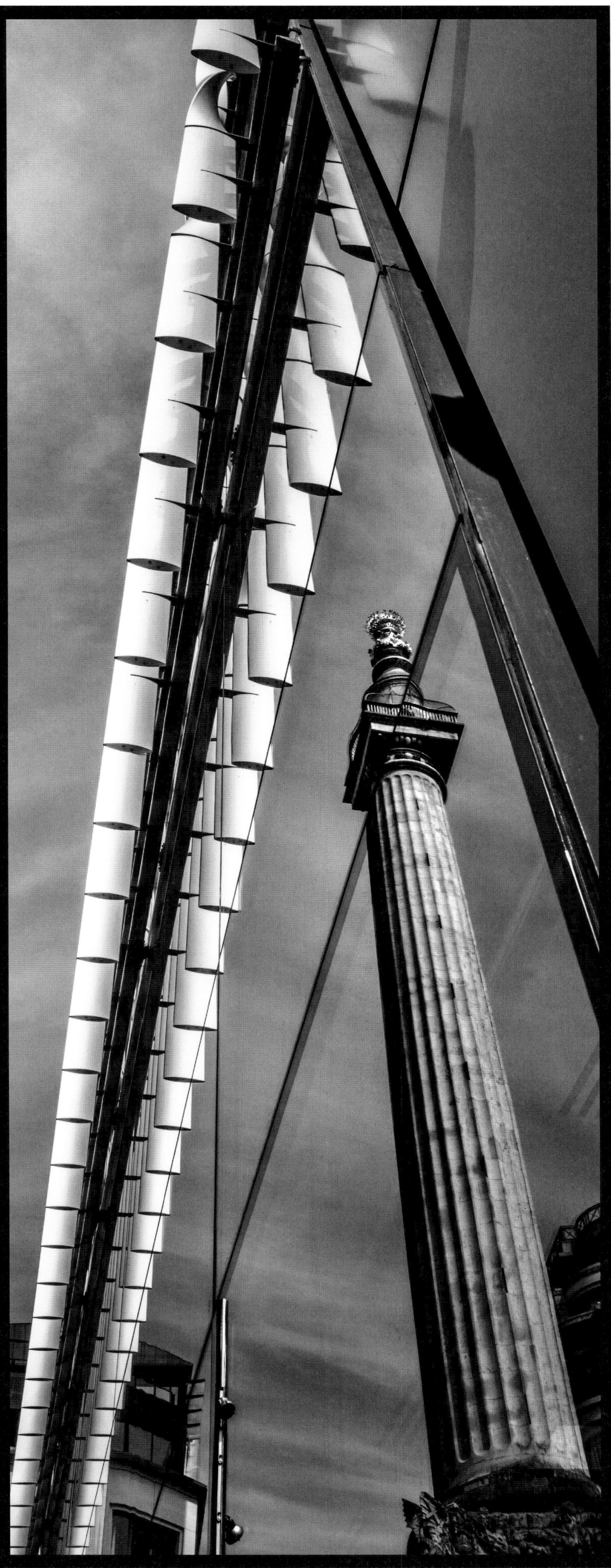

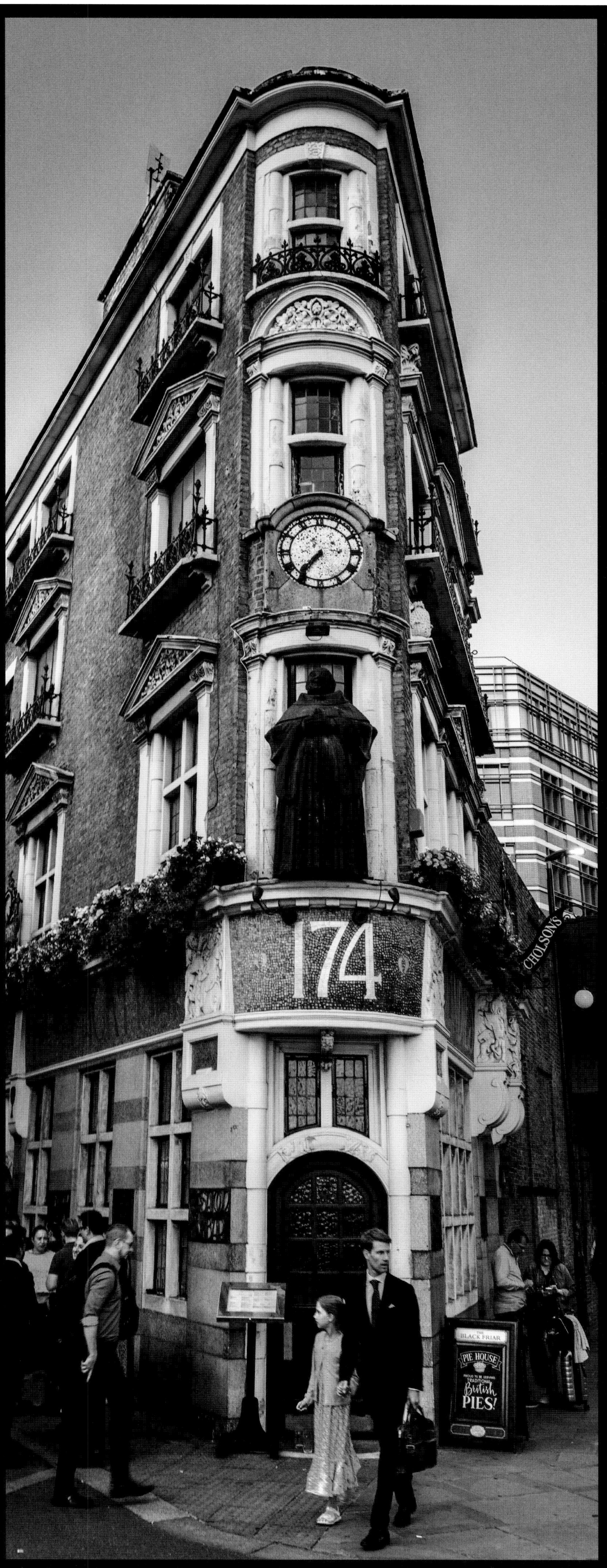
THE BLACK FRIAR
PIE HOUSE
PROUD TO BE SERVING
TRADITIONAL
British
PIES!
NICHOLSON'S
174
THE BLACK FRIAR
PIE HOUSE
PROUD TO BE SERVING
TRADITIONAL
British
PIES!

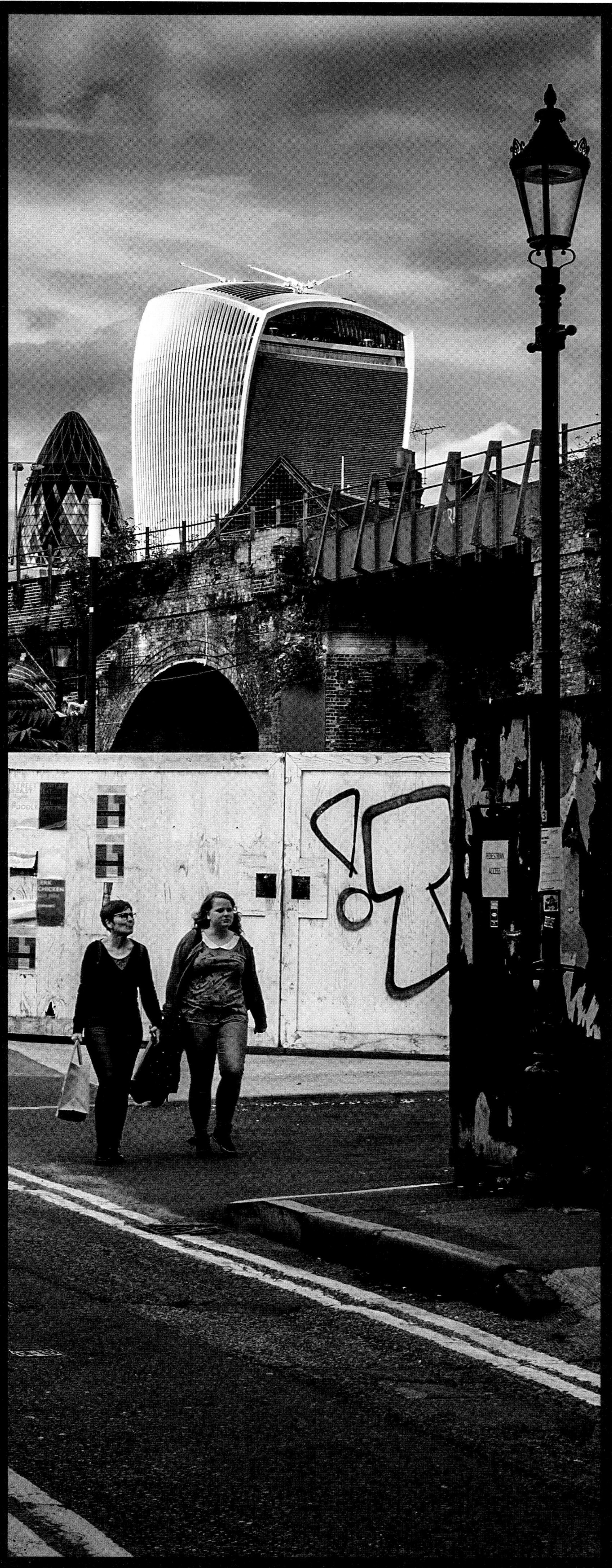

The Fenchurch Building   38

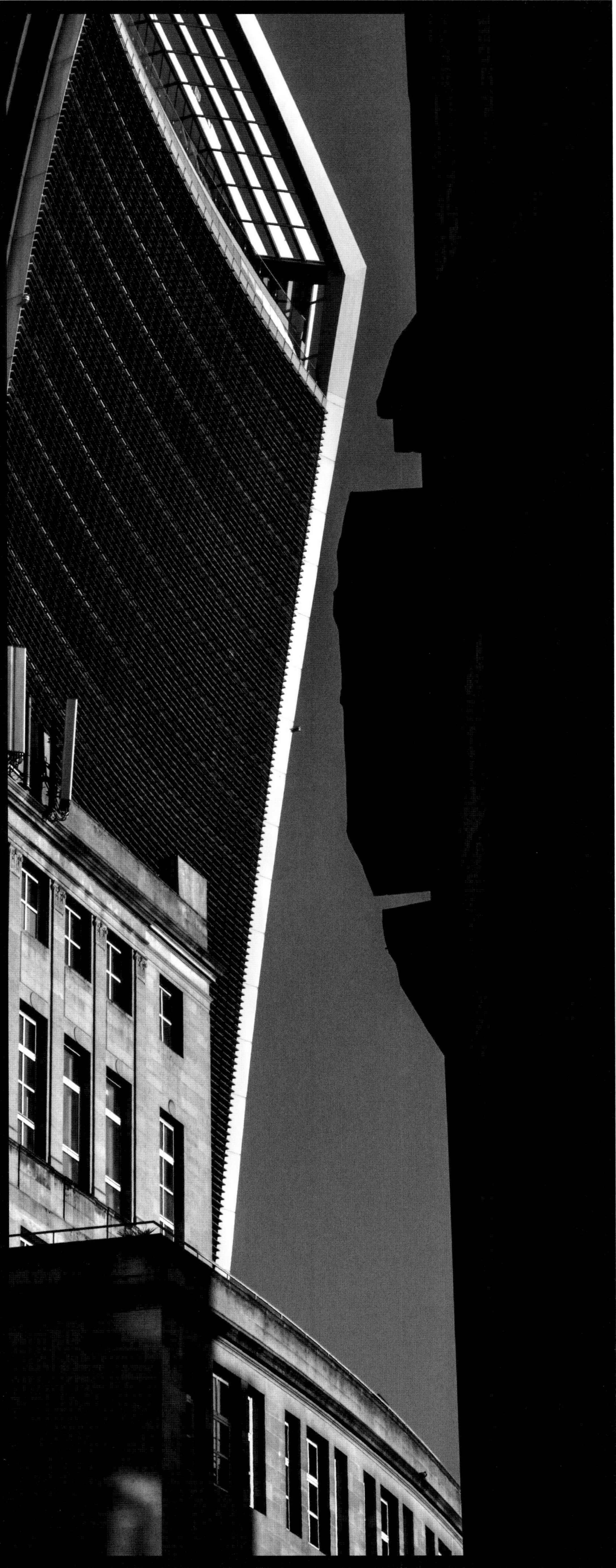

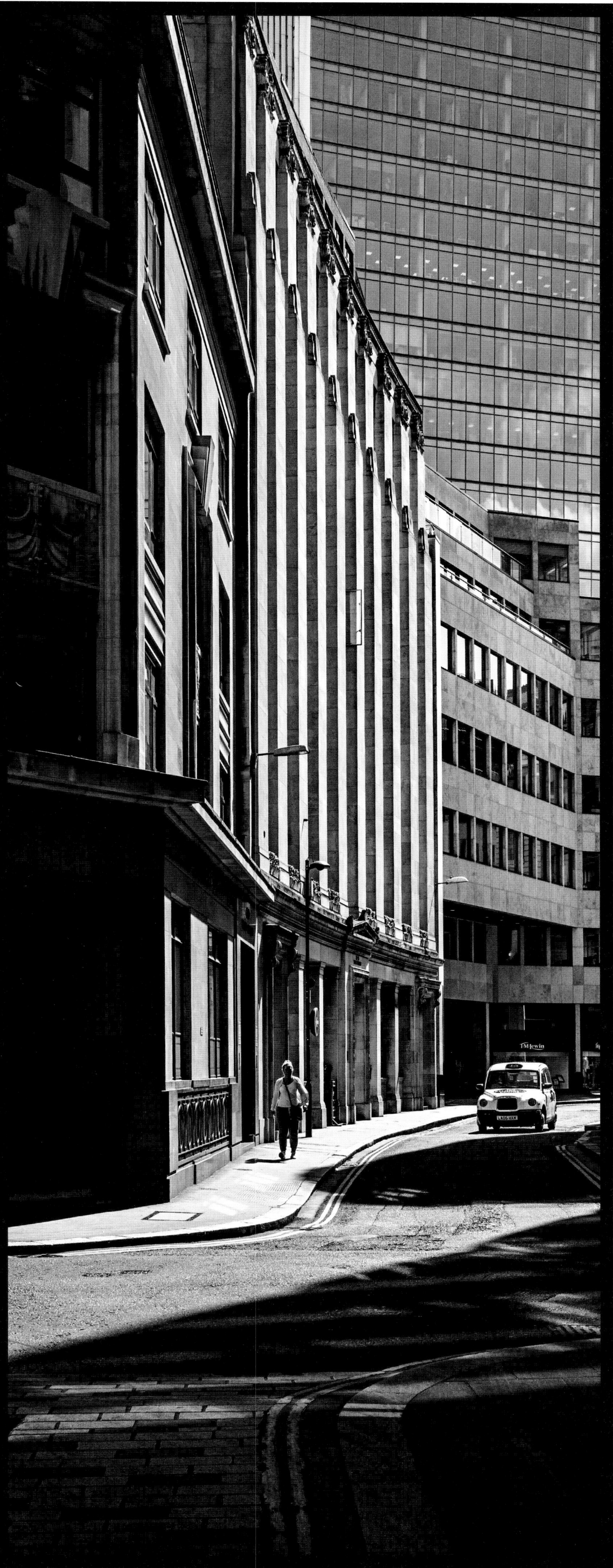

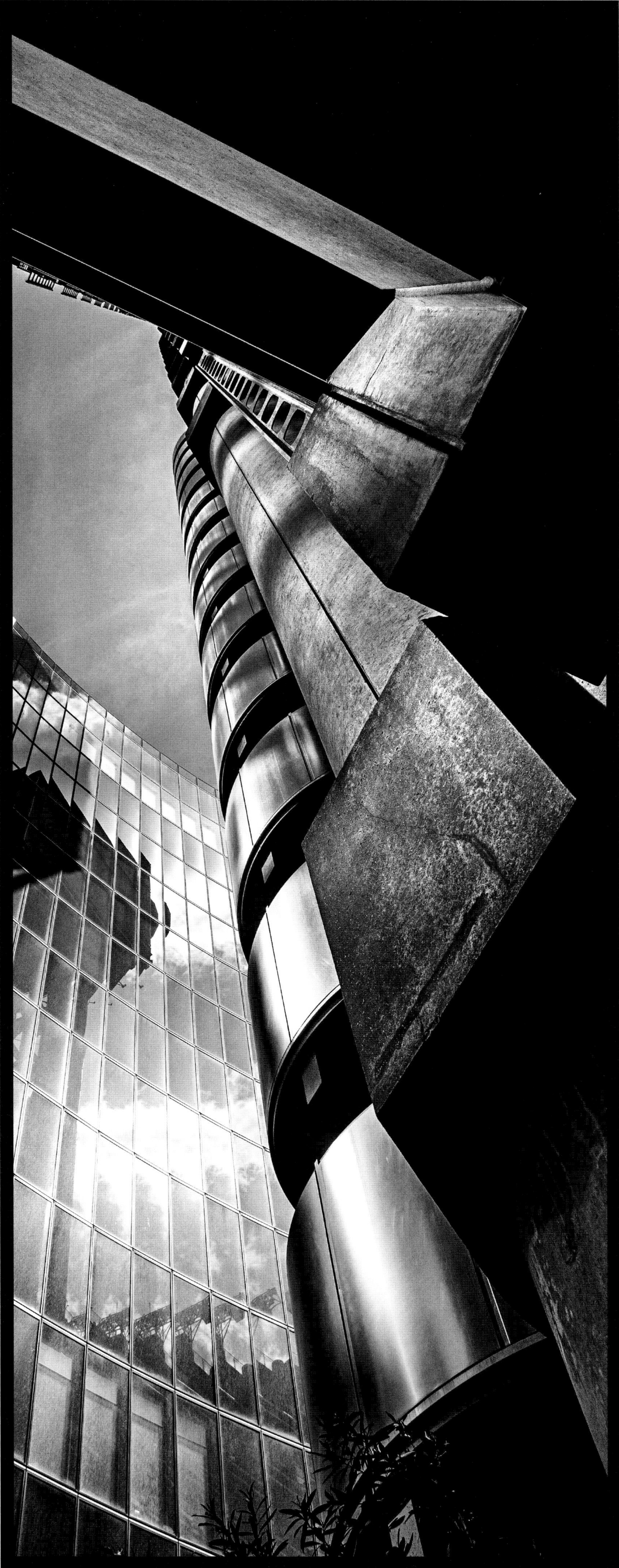

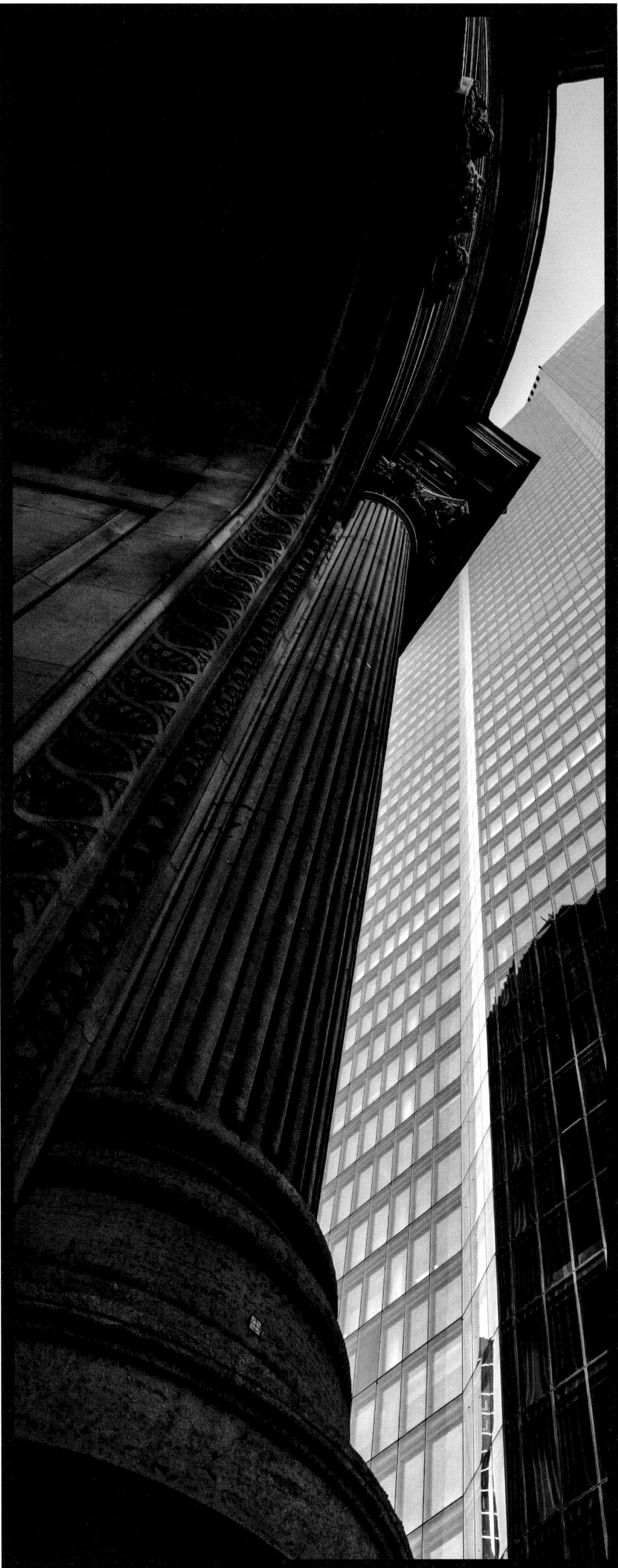

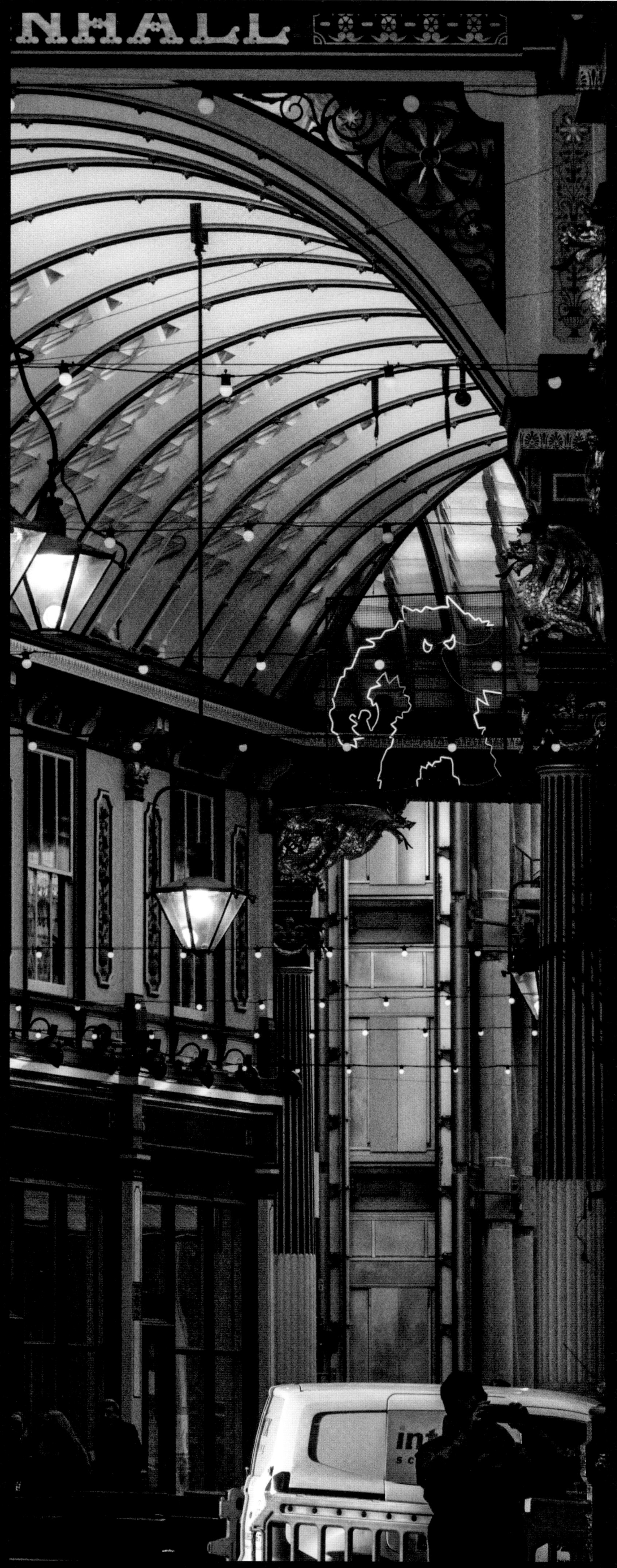

NHALL

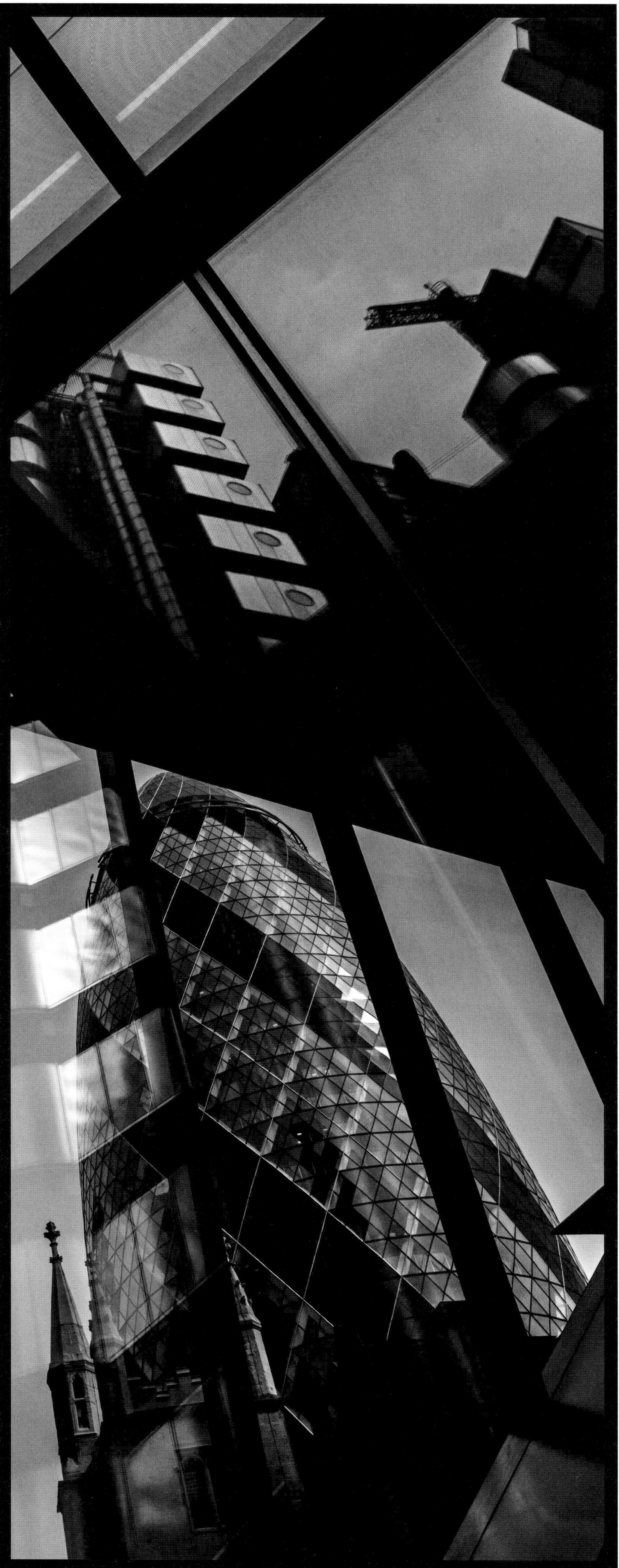

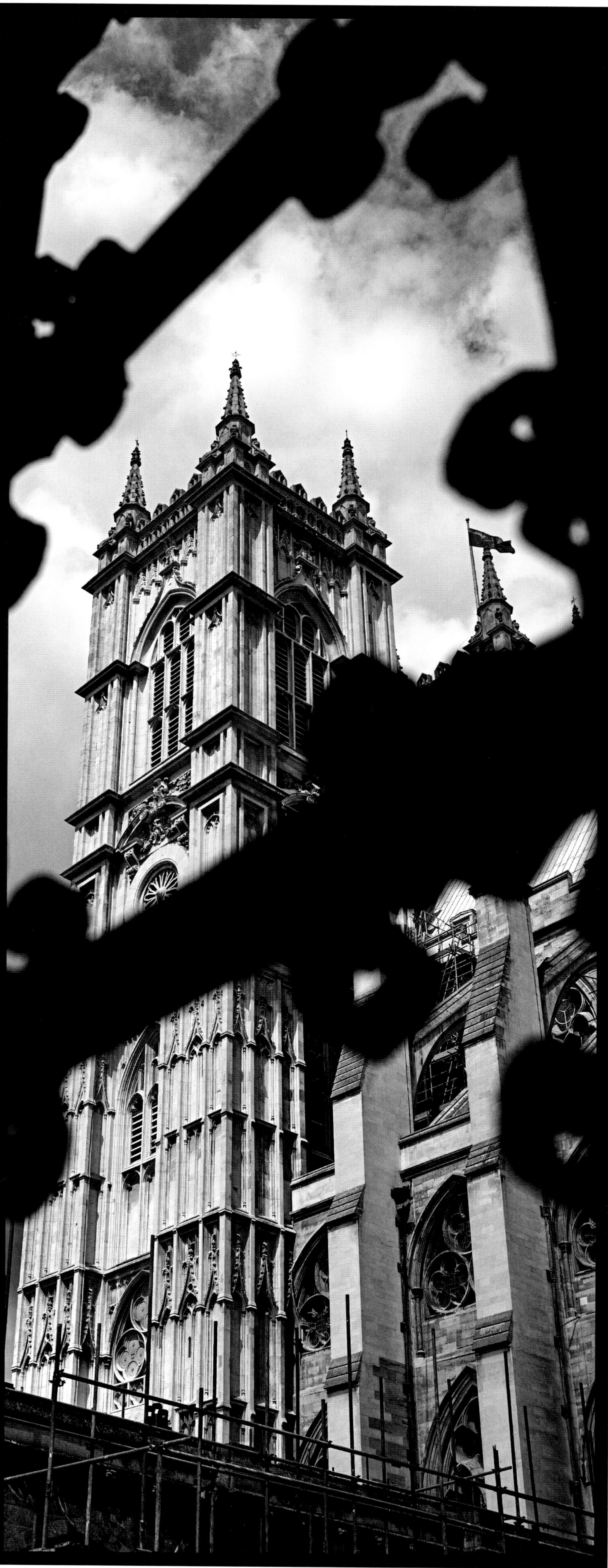

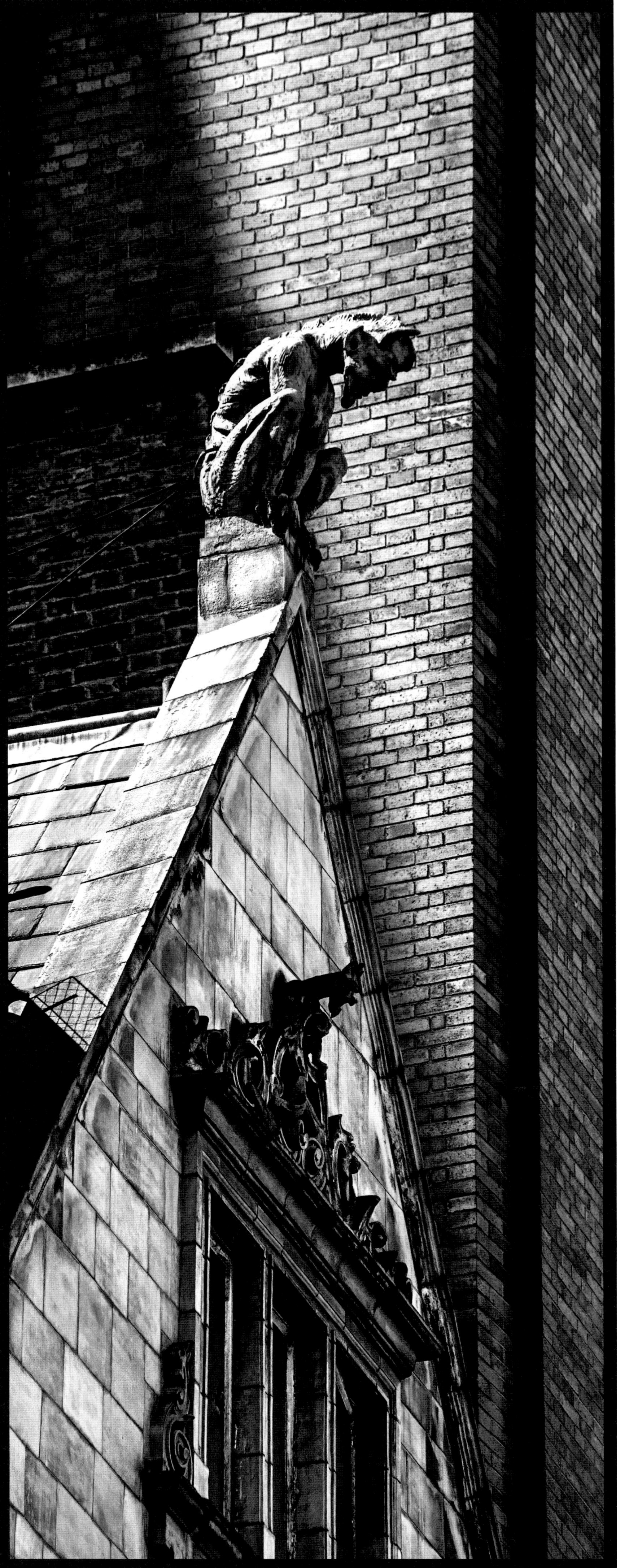

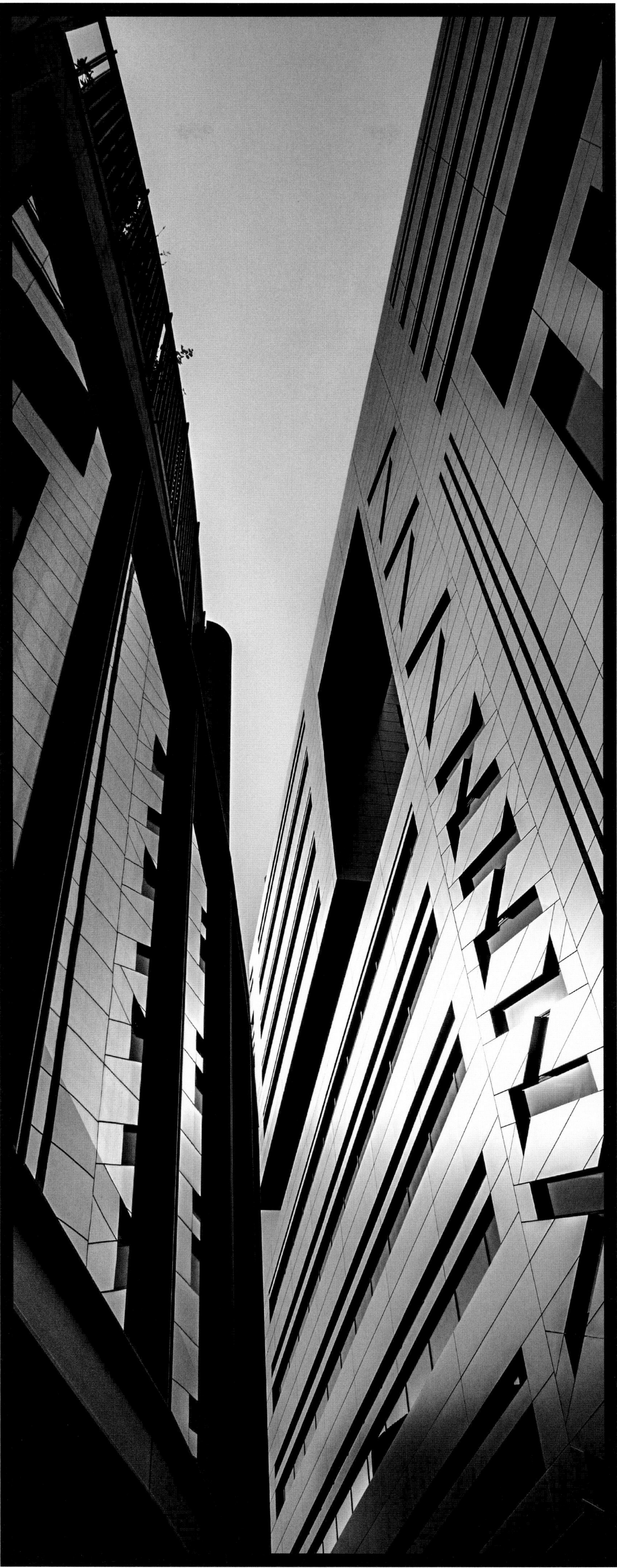

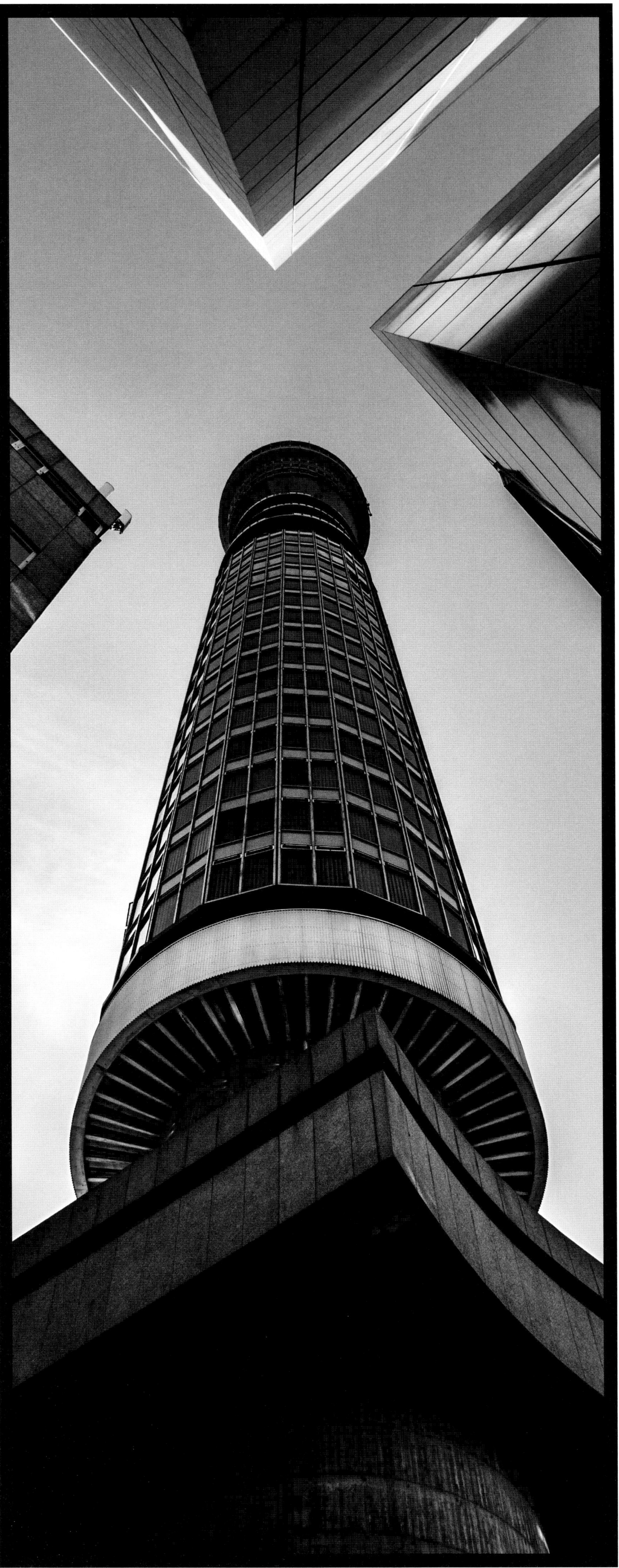

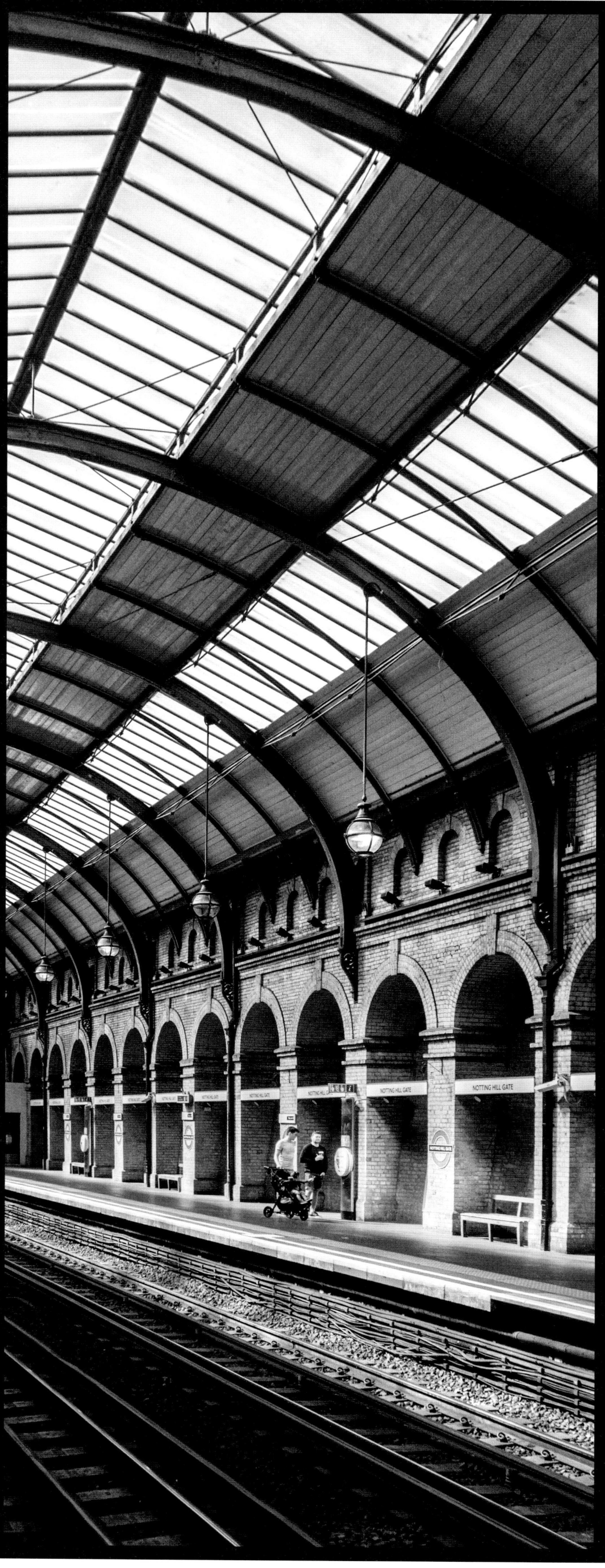

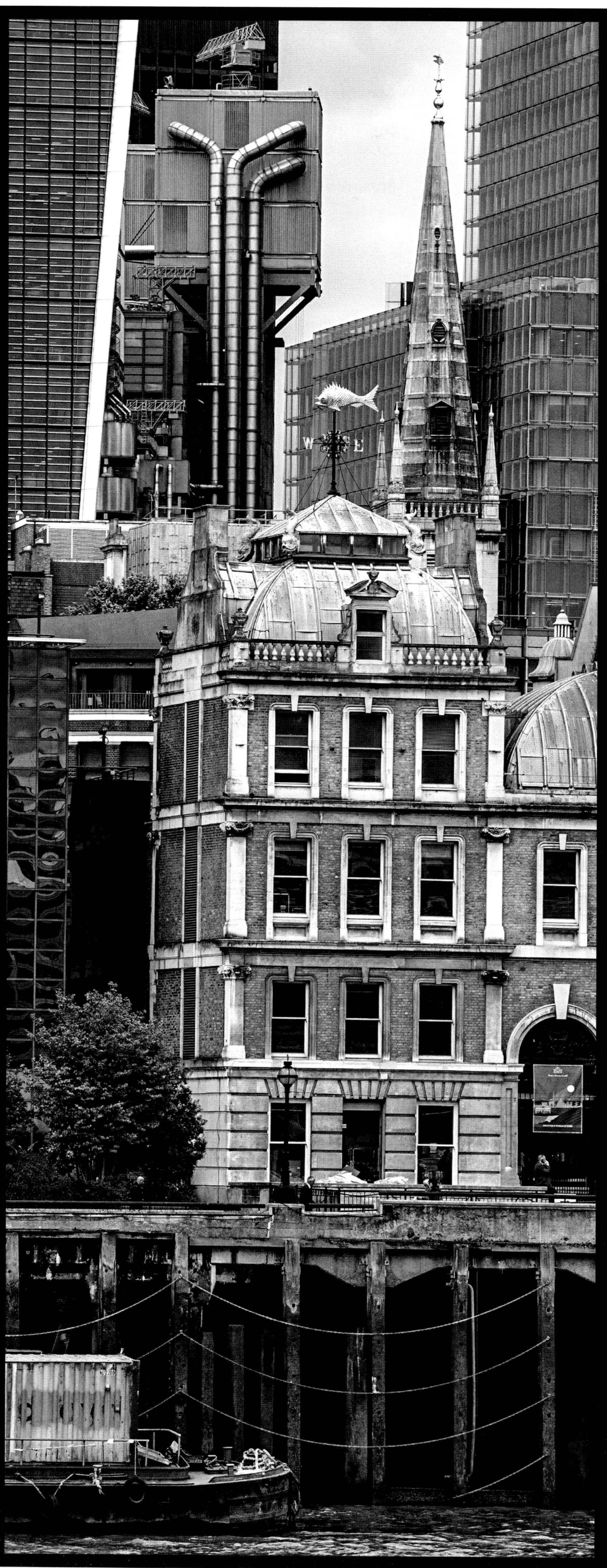

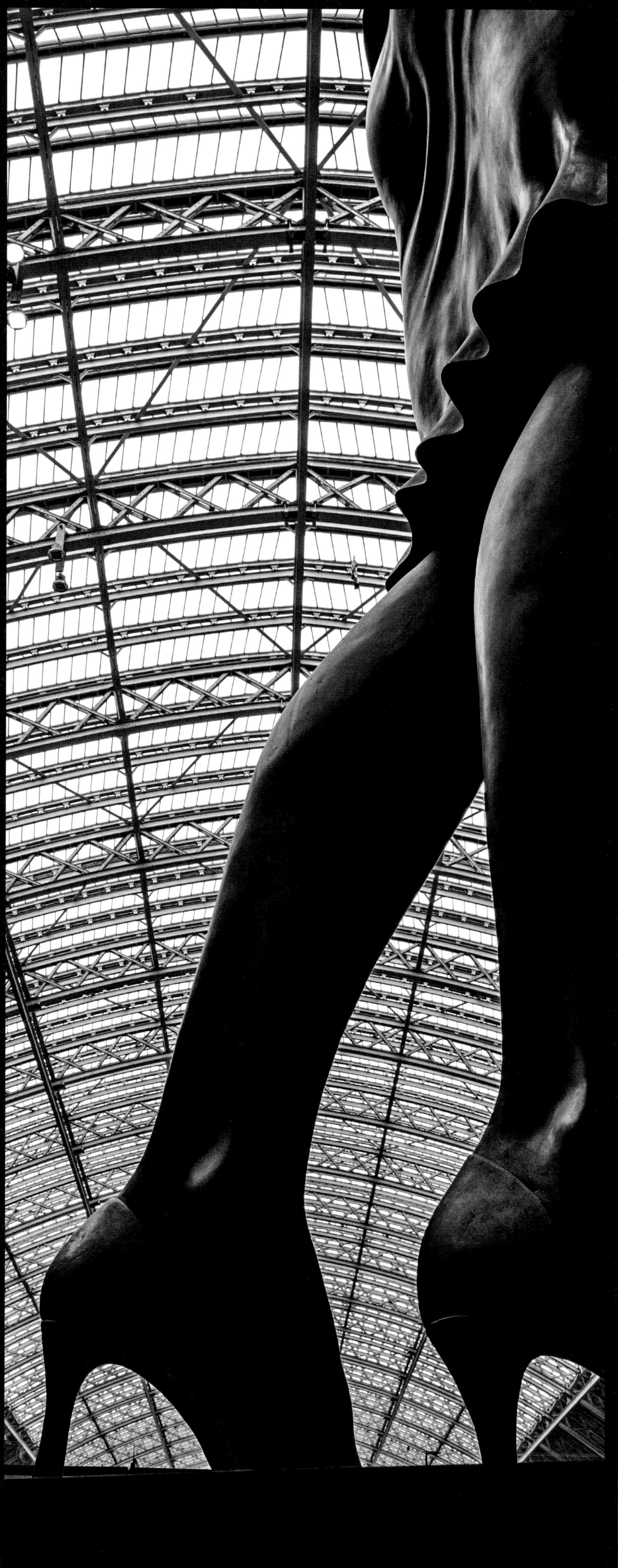

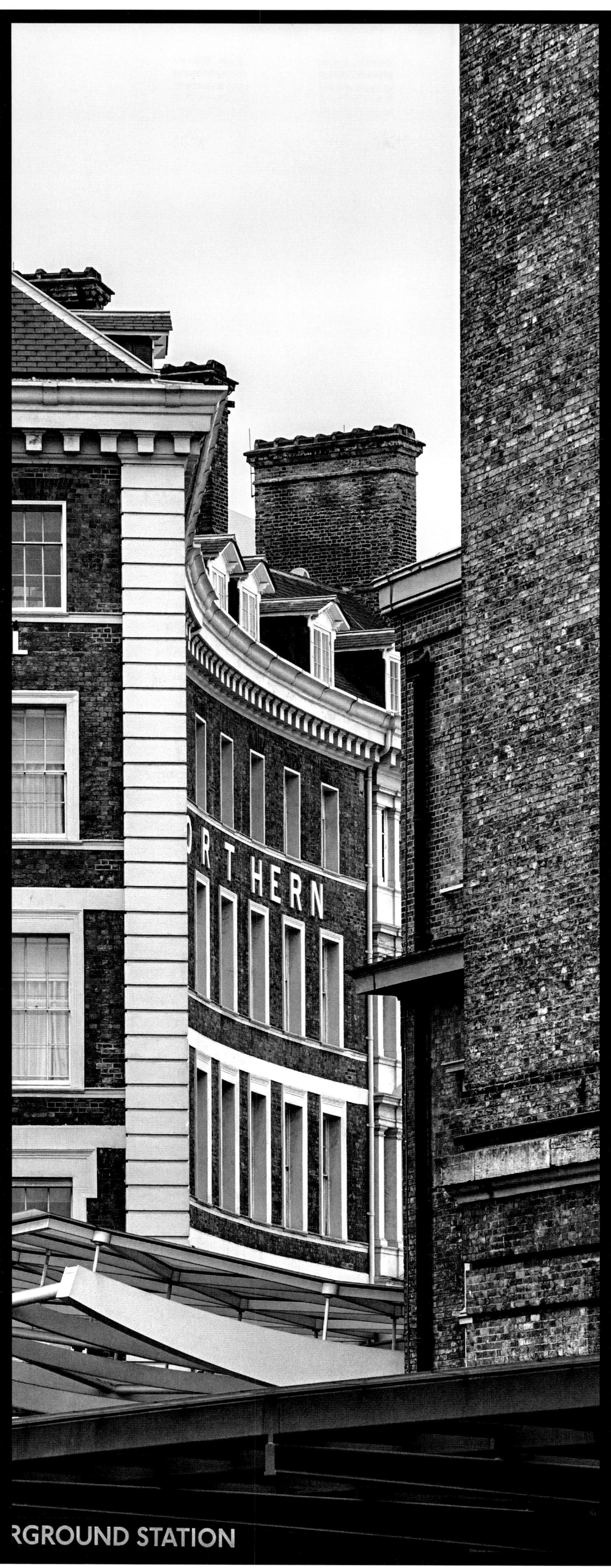
ORTHERN
RGROUND STATION

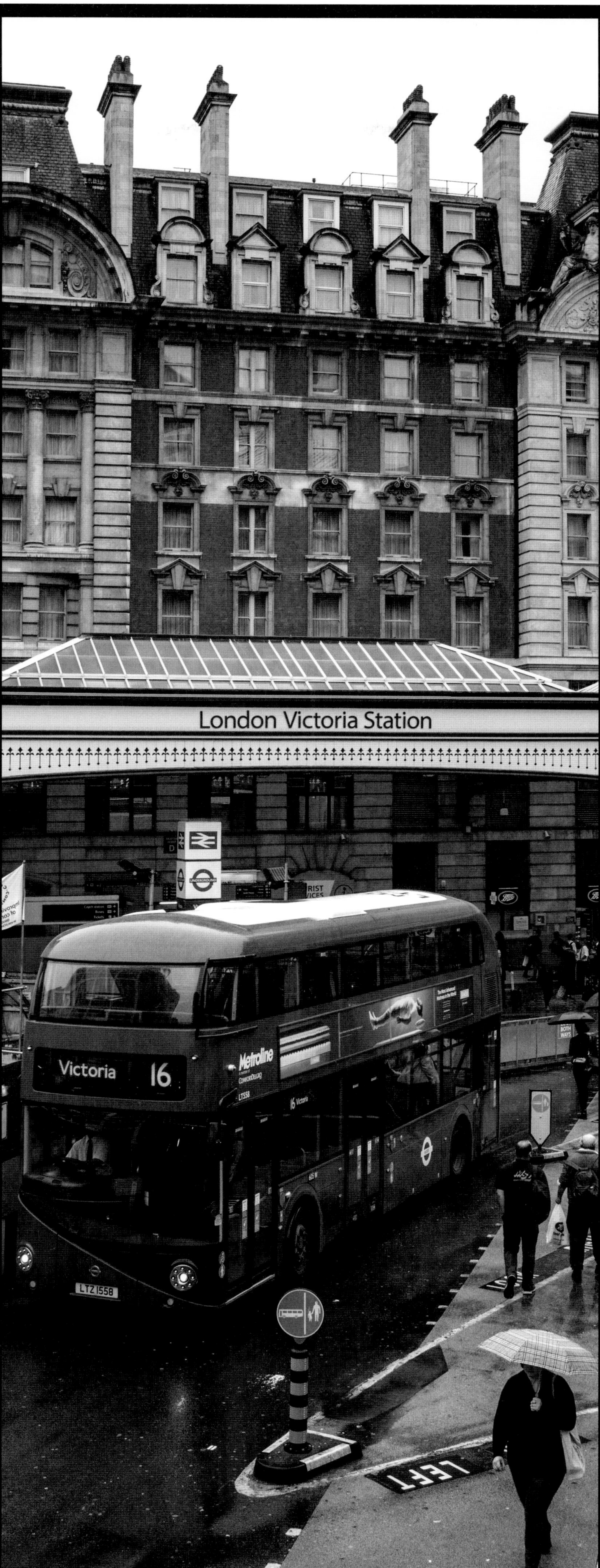

London Victoria Station
Victoria 16
Metroline
Victoria
LTZ 1558
LEFT

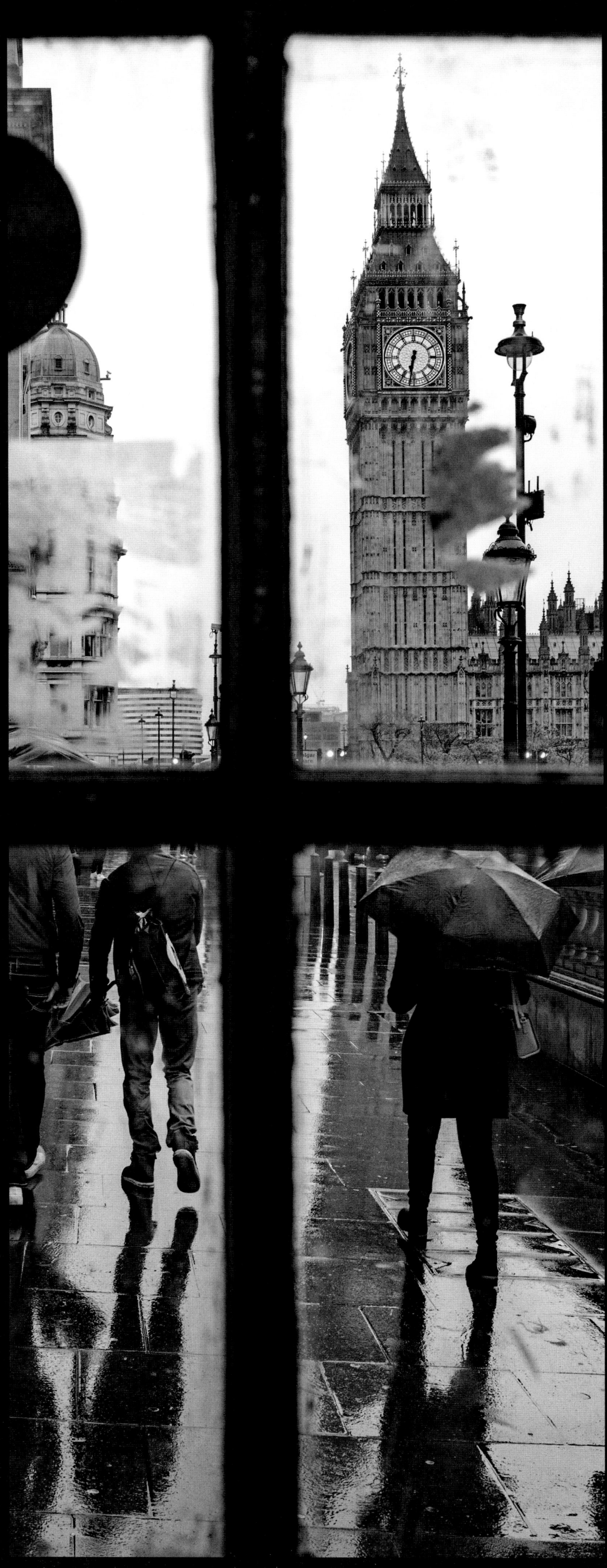

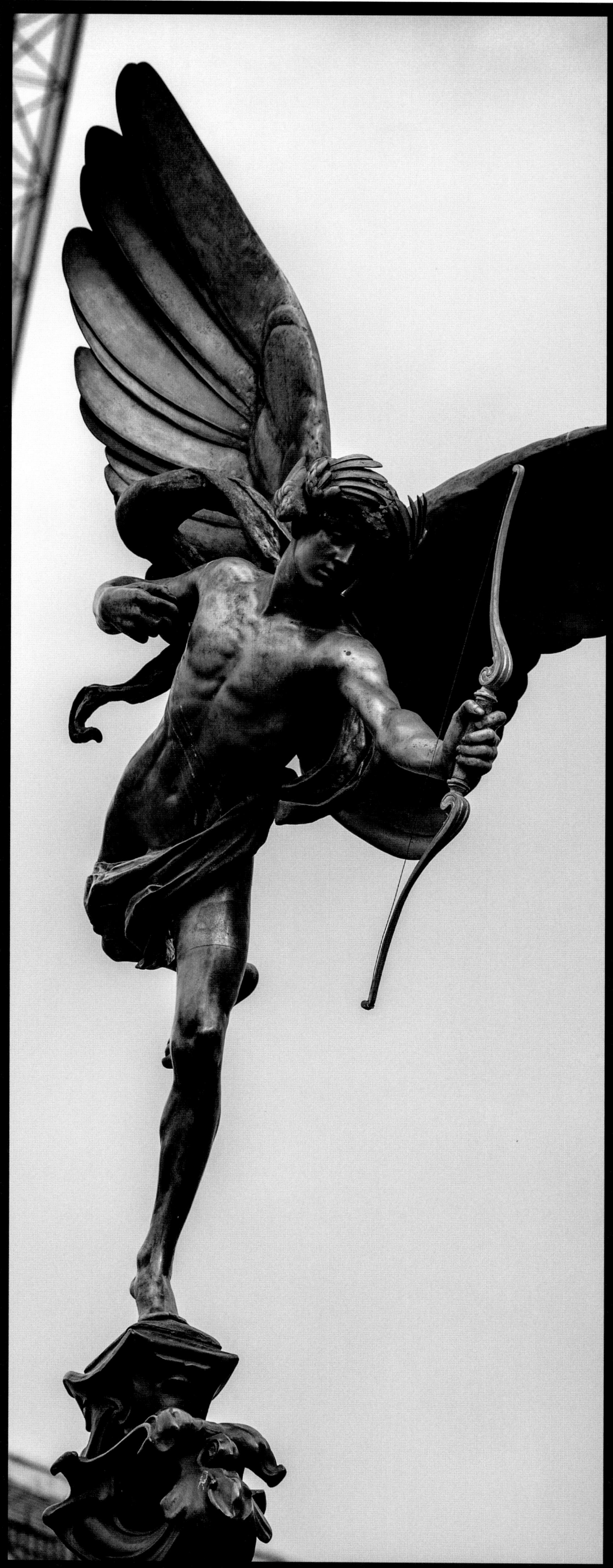

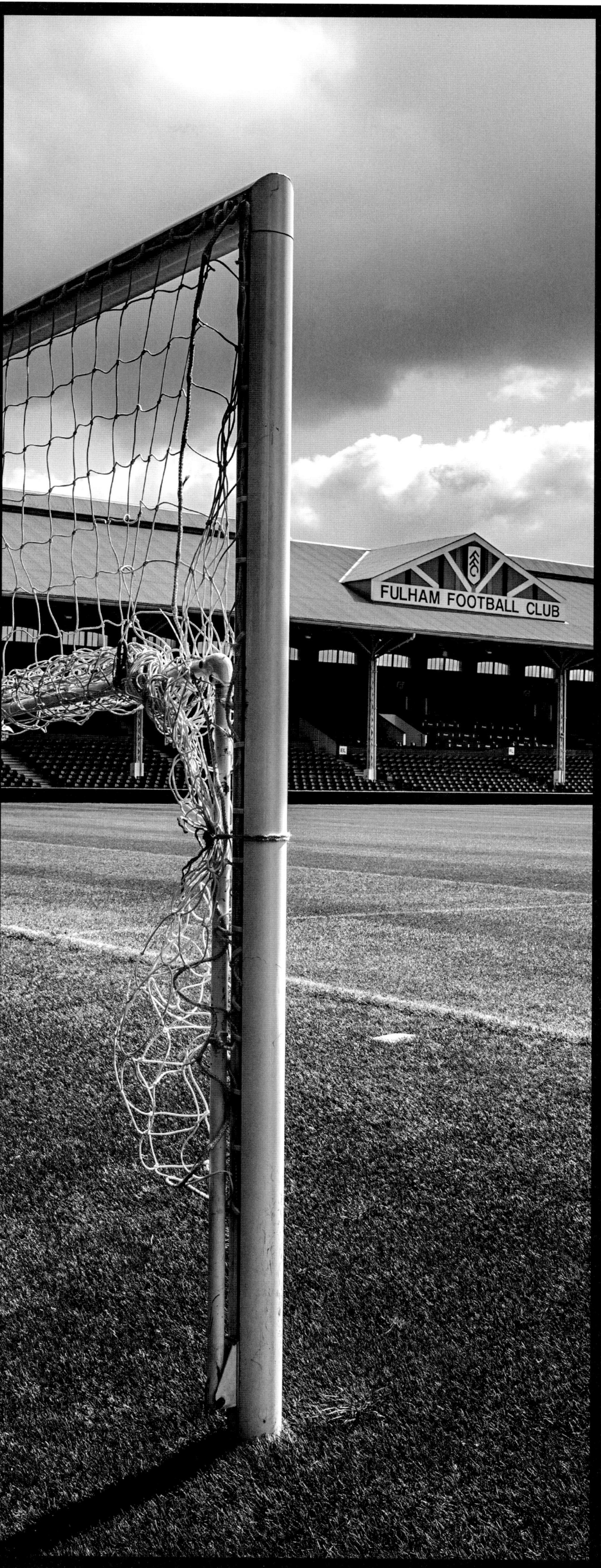
FULHAM FOOTBALL CLUB

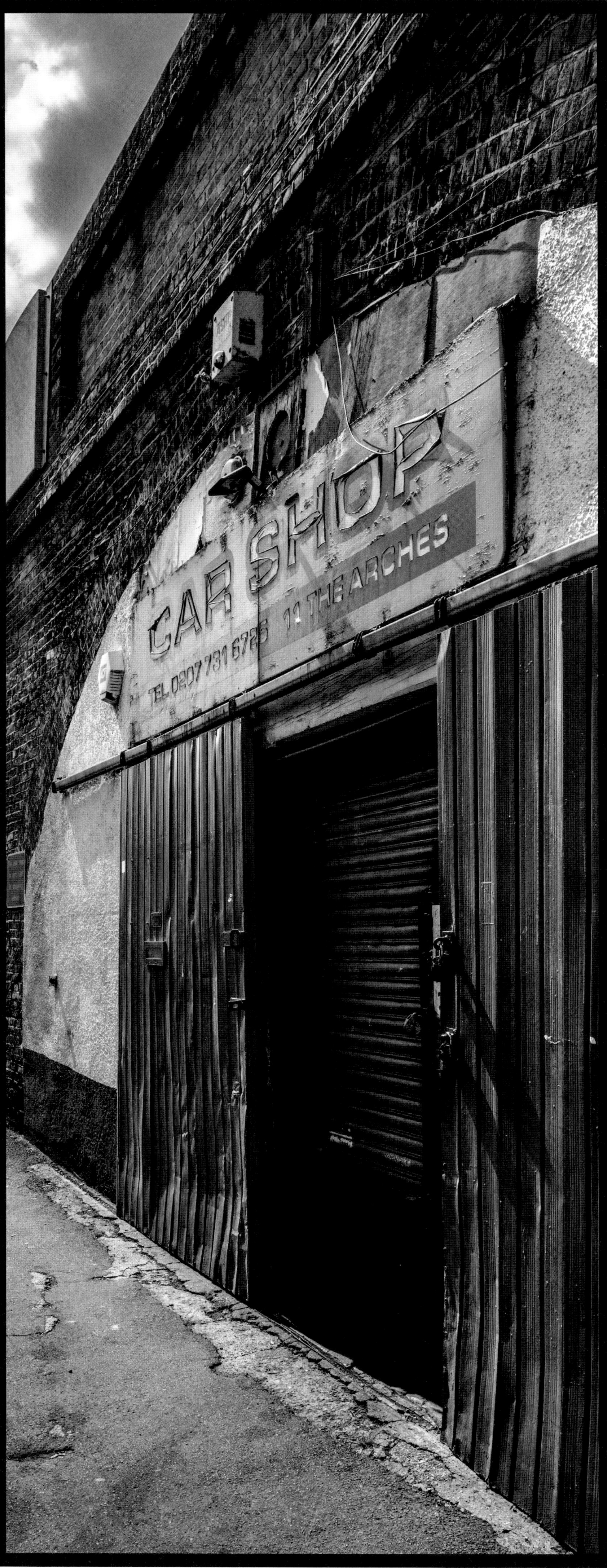

CAR SHOP
TEL. 0207 731 6726   11 THE ARCHES

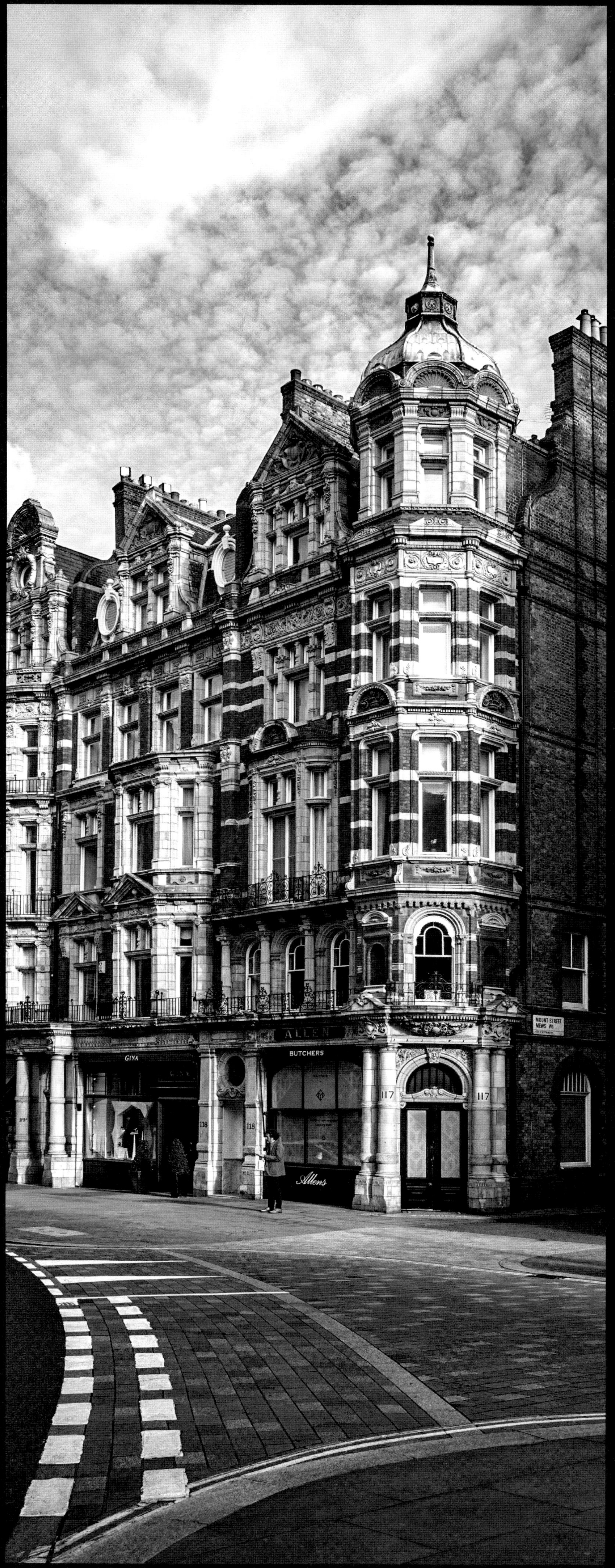

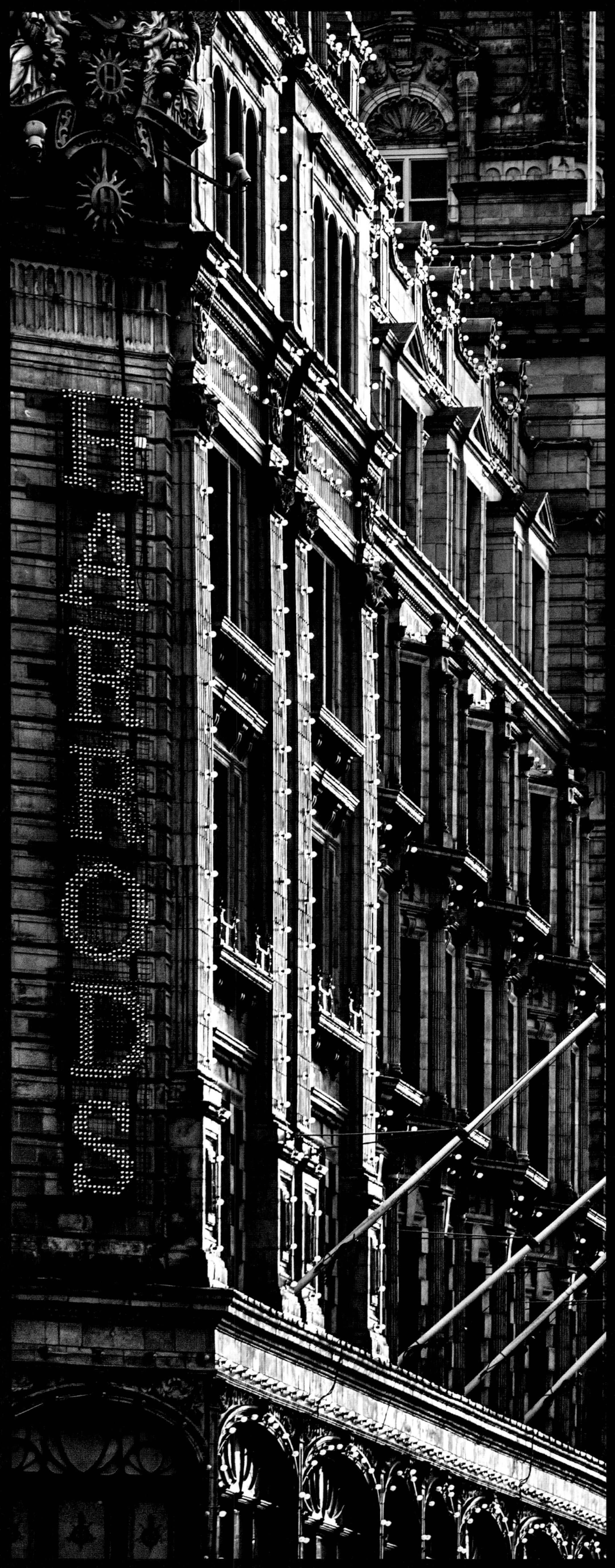

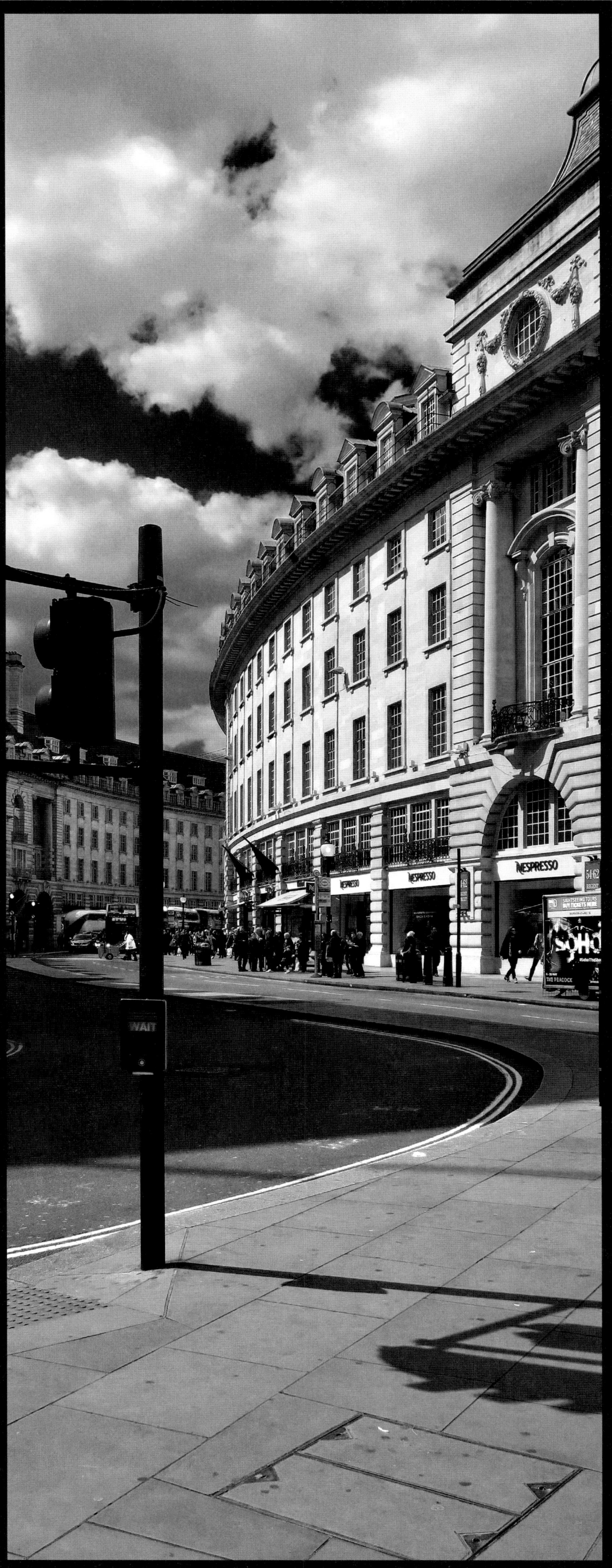

WAIT
NESPRESSO
NESPRESSO

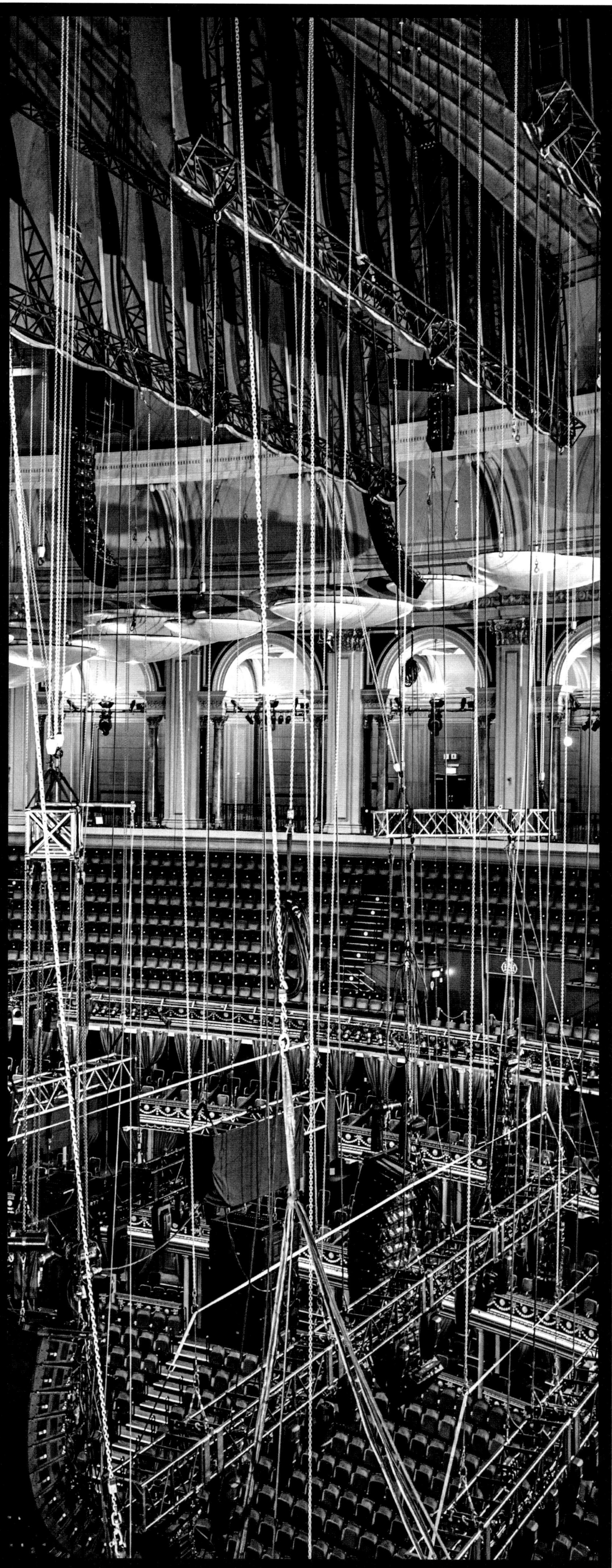

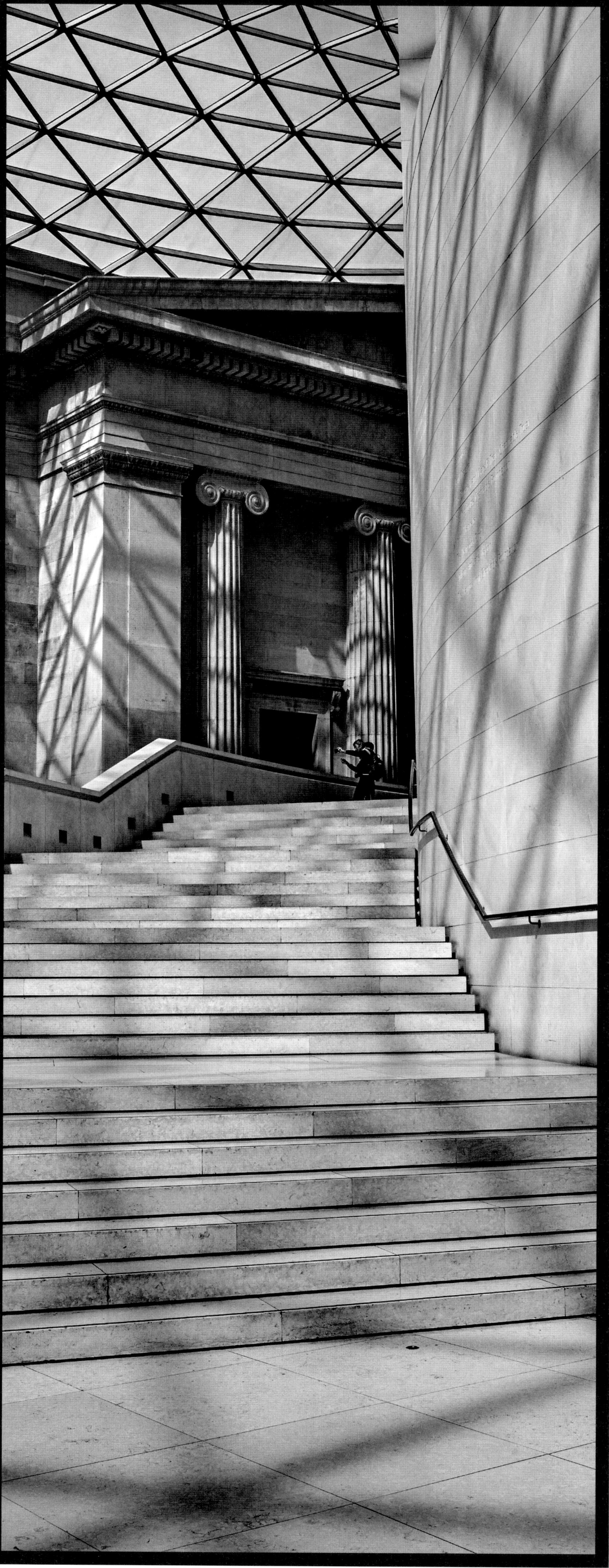

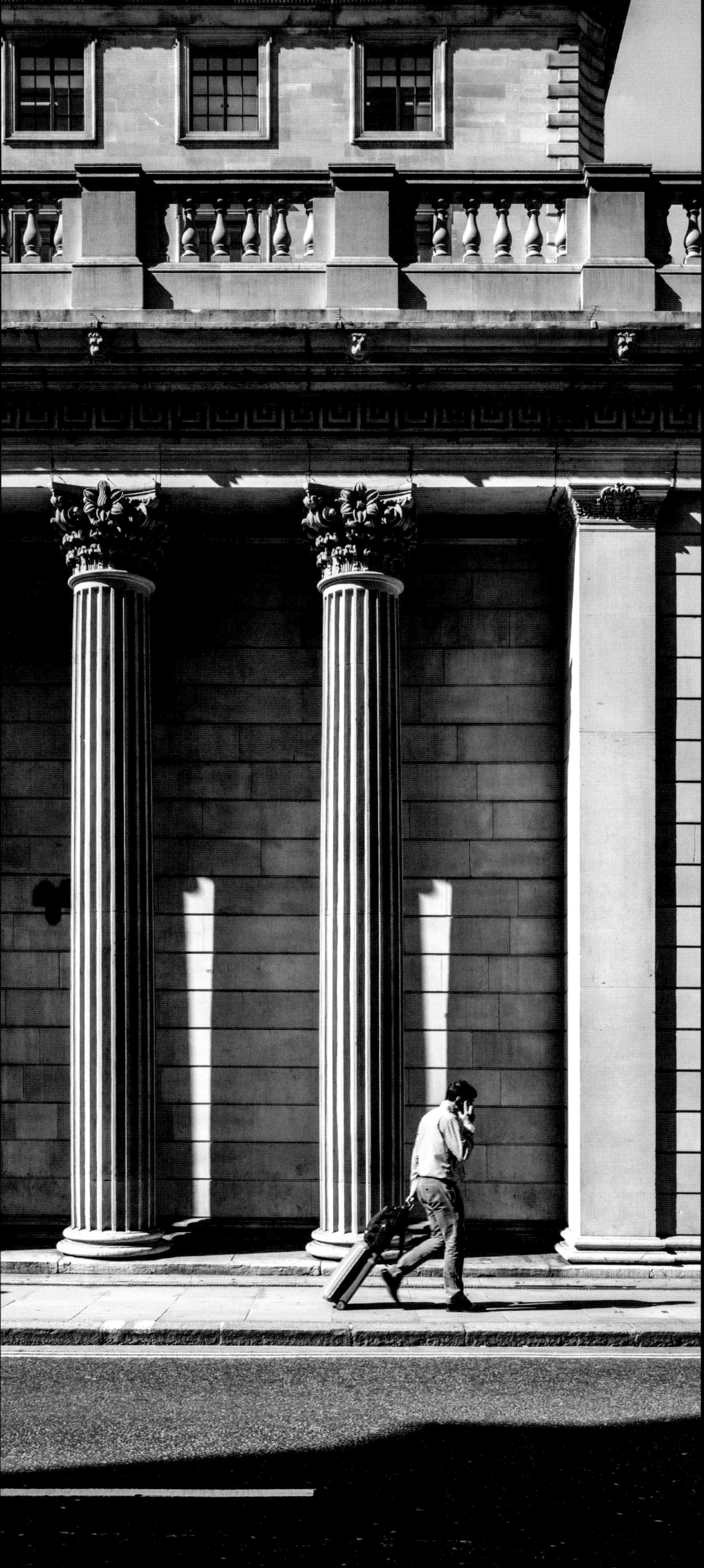

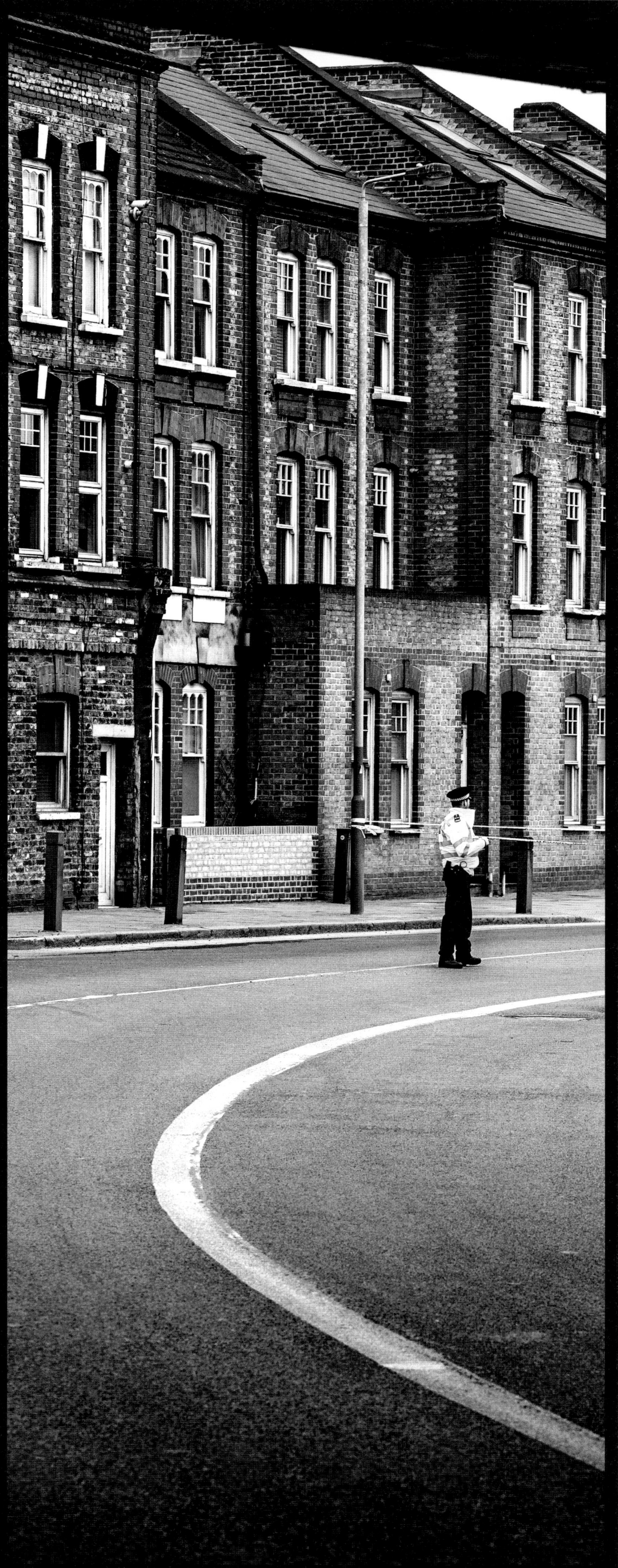

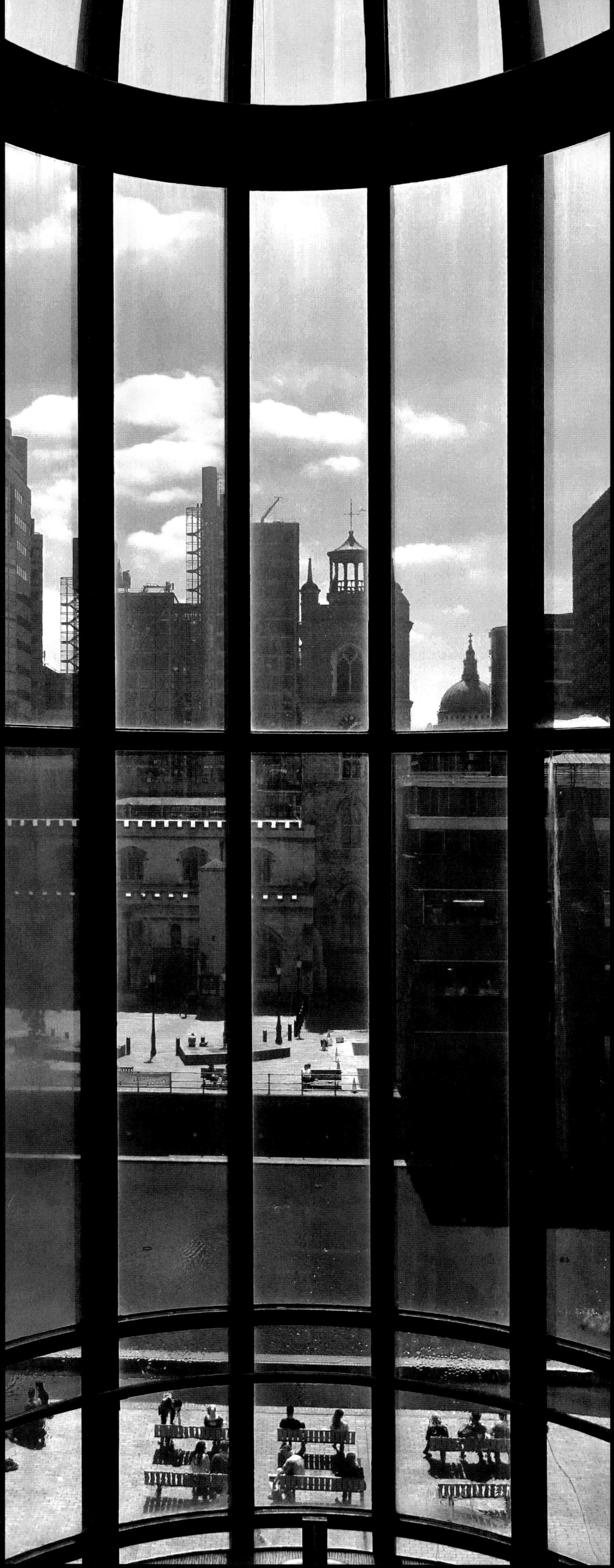

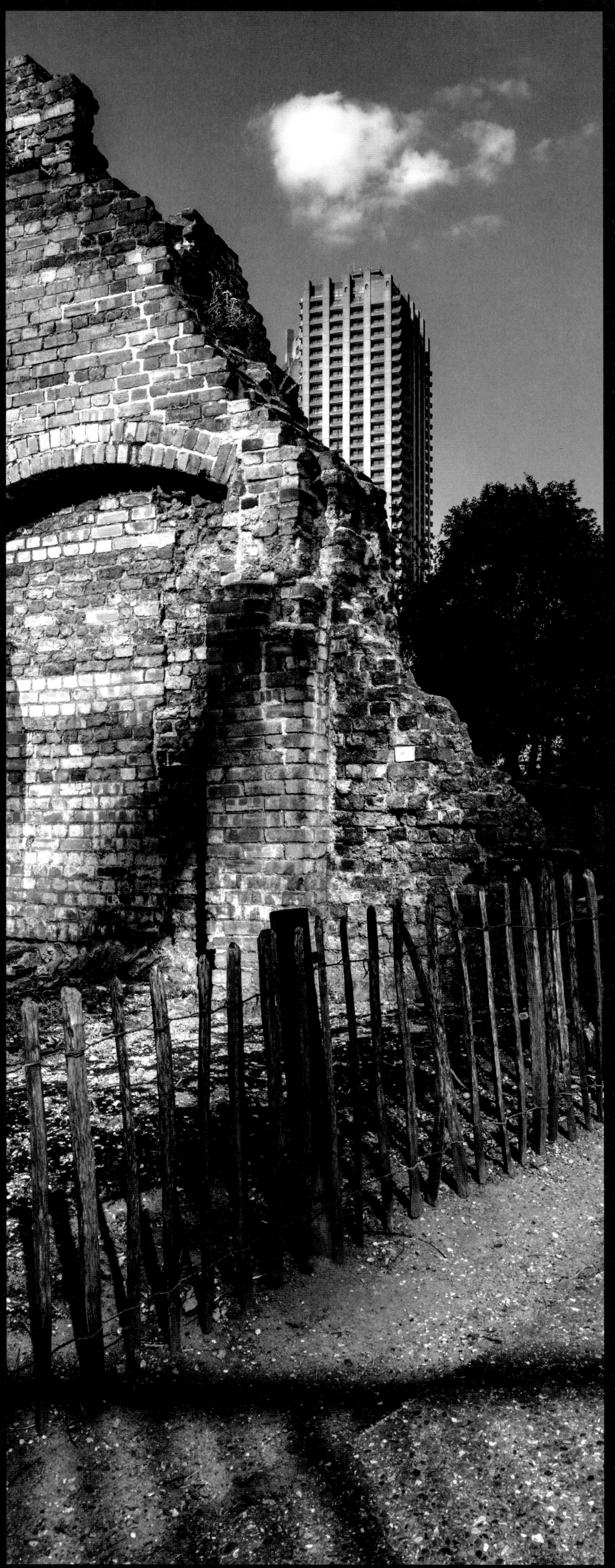

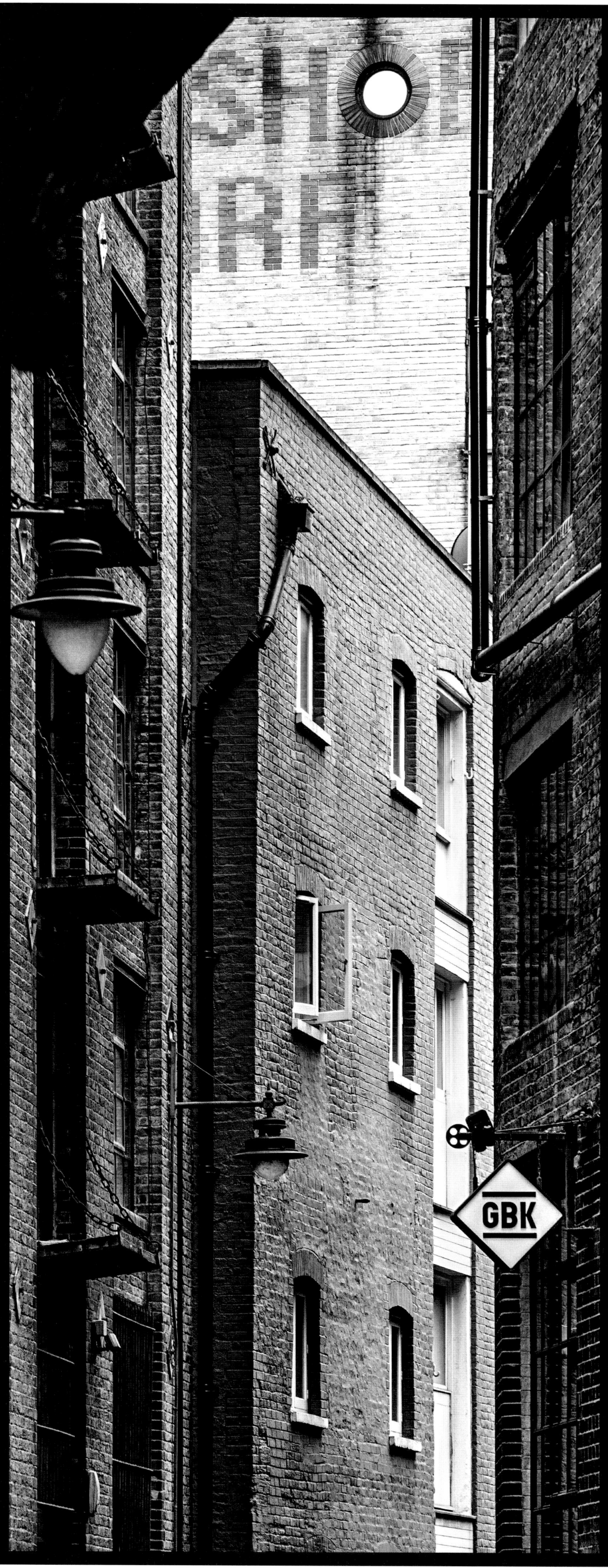

GBK

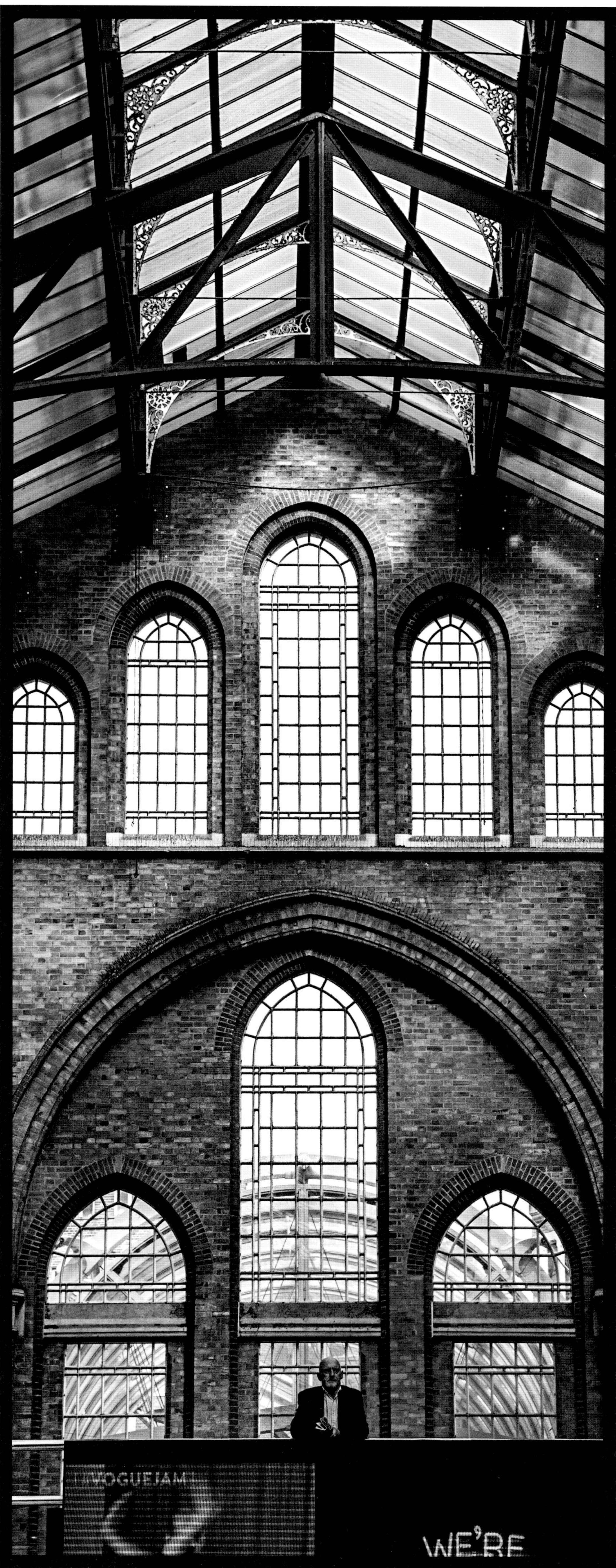
VOGUEJAM
WE'RE

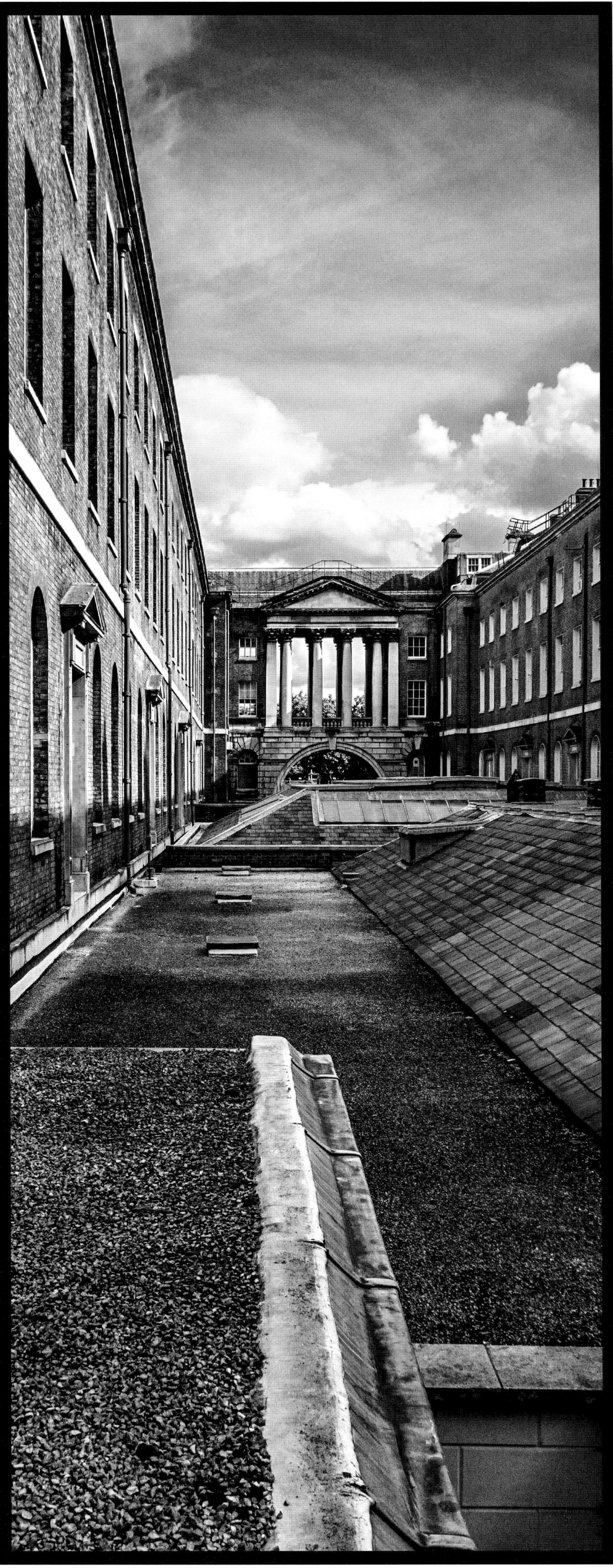

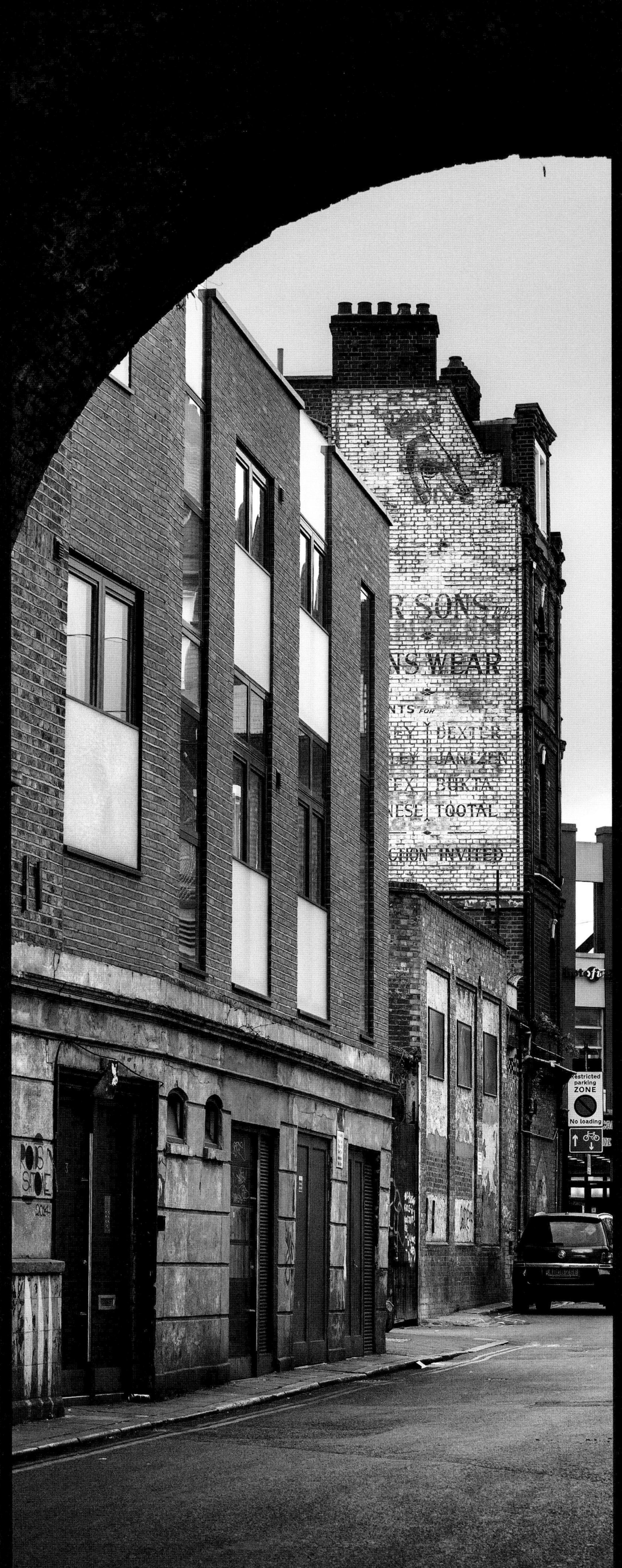
R SONS
NS WEAR
NTS FOR
EY DEXTER
EY JANZEN
EX BUKTA
NESE TOOTAL
CTION INVITED
ROOS N
STORE
Restricted
parking
ZONE
No loading

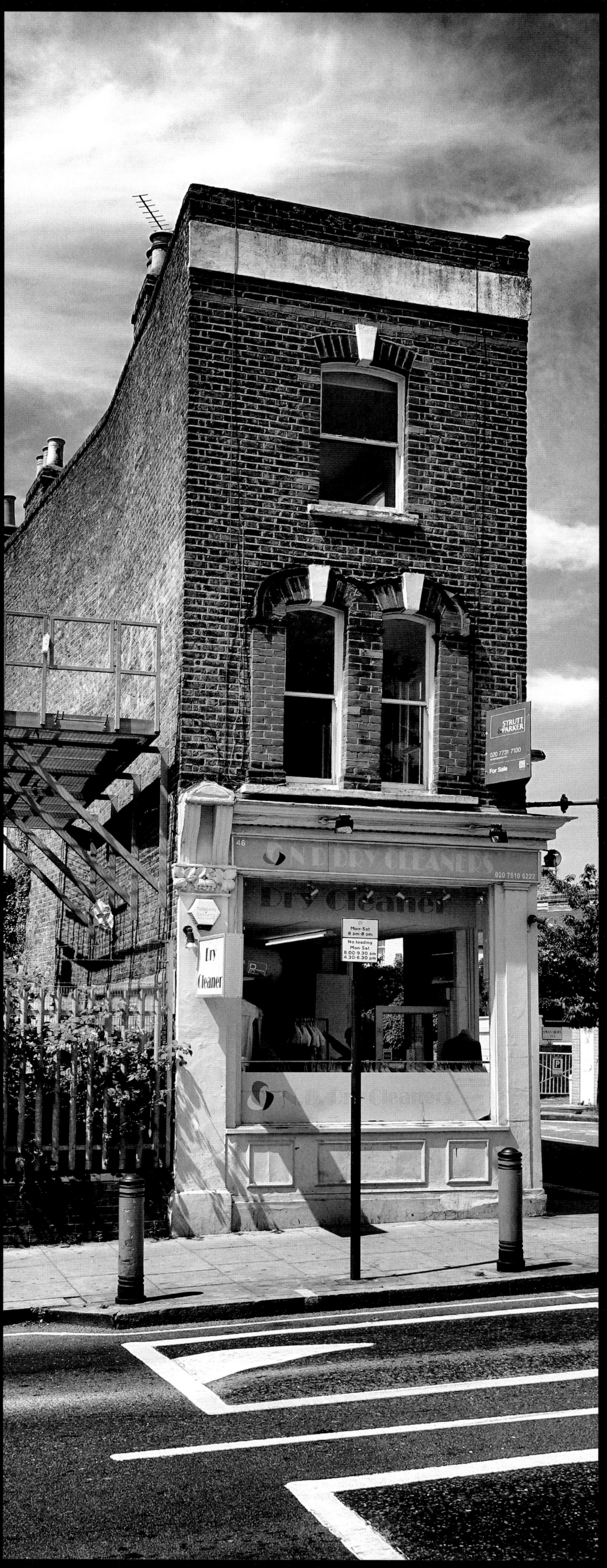

STRUTT & PARKER
020 7731 7100
For Sale
46
DRY CLEANERS
020 7610 6222
Dry Cleaner
Telecom Security
Dry Cleaner
Mon-Sat
8 am-8 pm
No loading
Mon-Sat
8.00-9.30 am
4.30-6.30 pm

Battersea Power Station   104

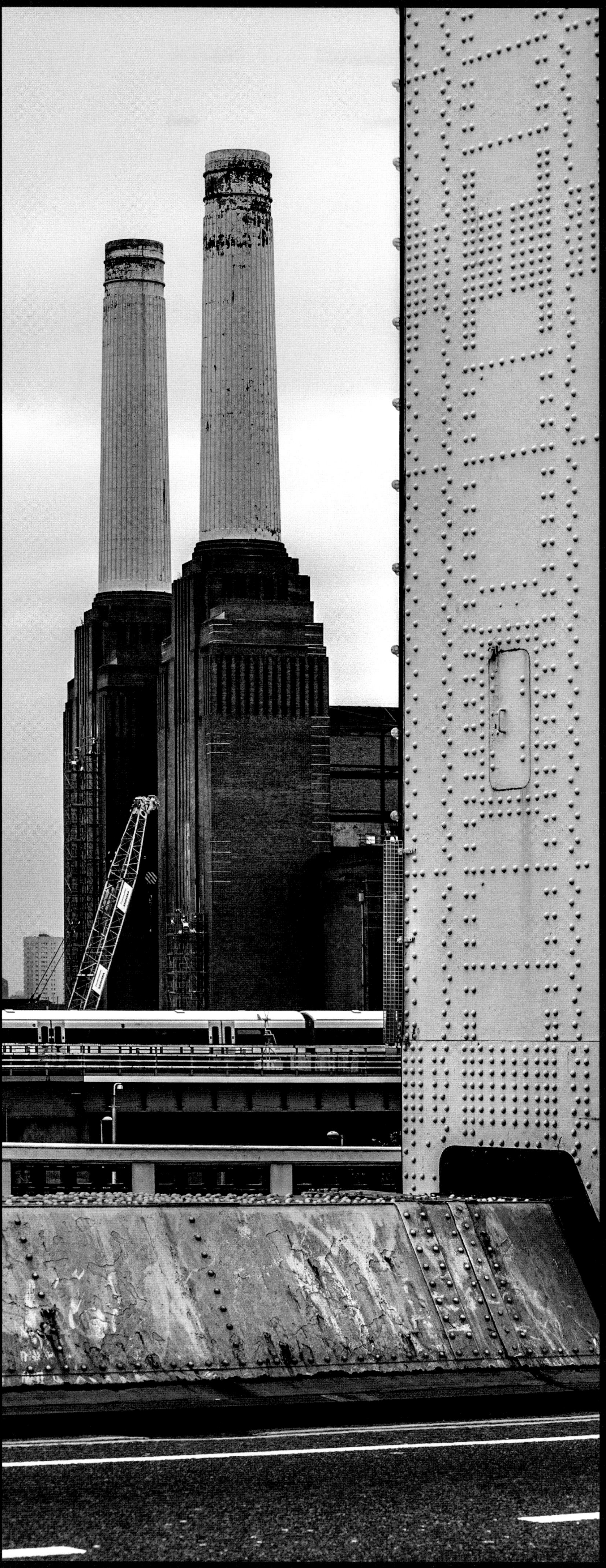

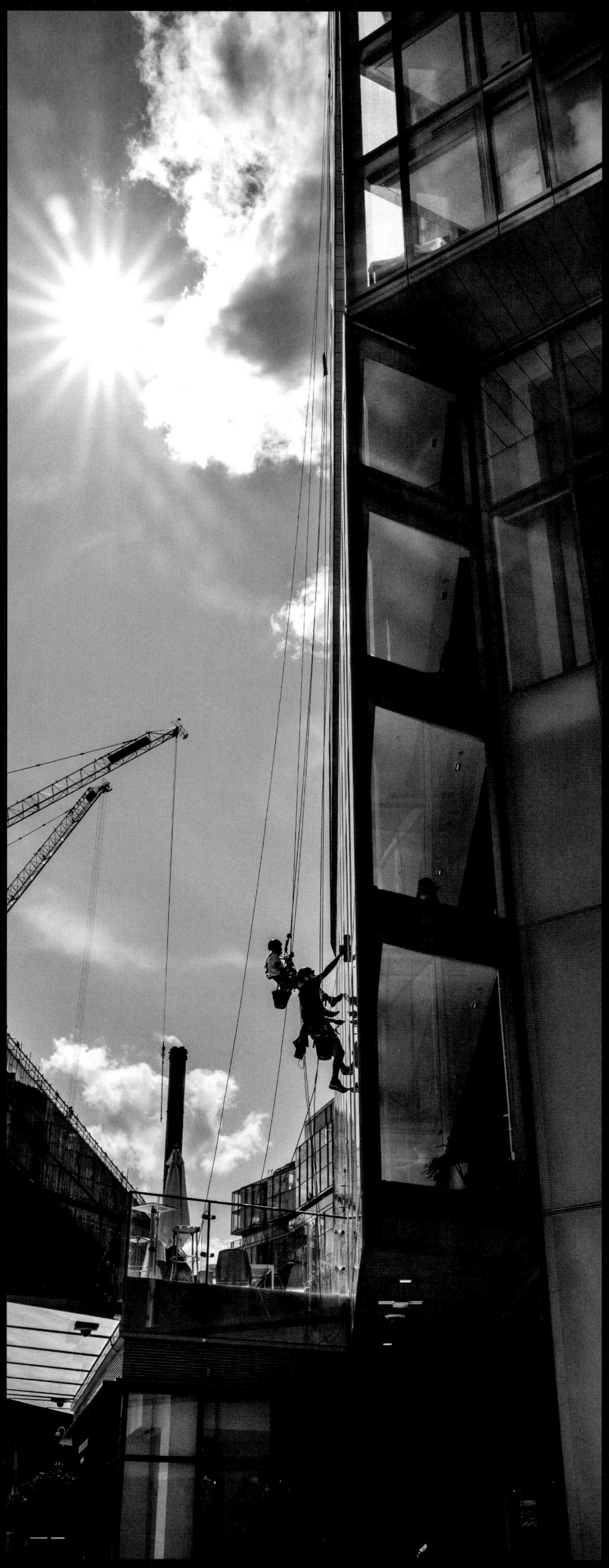

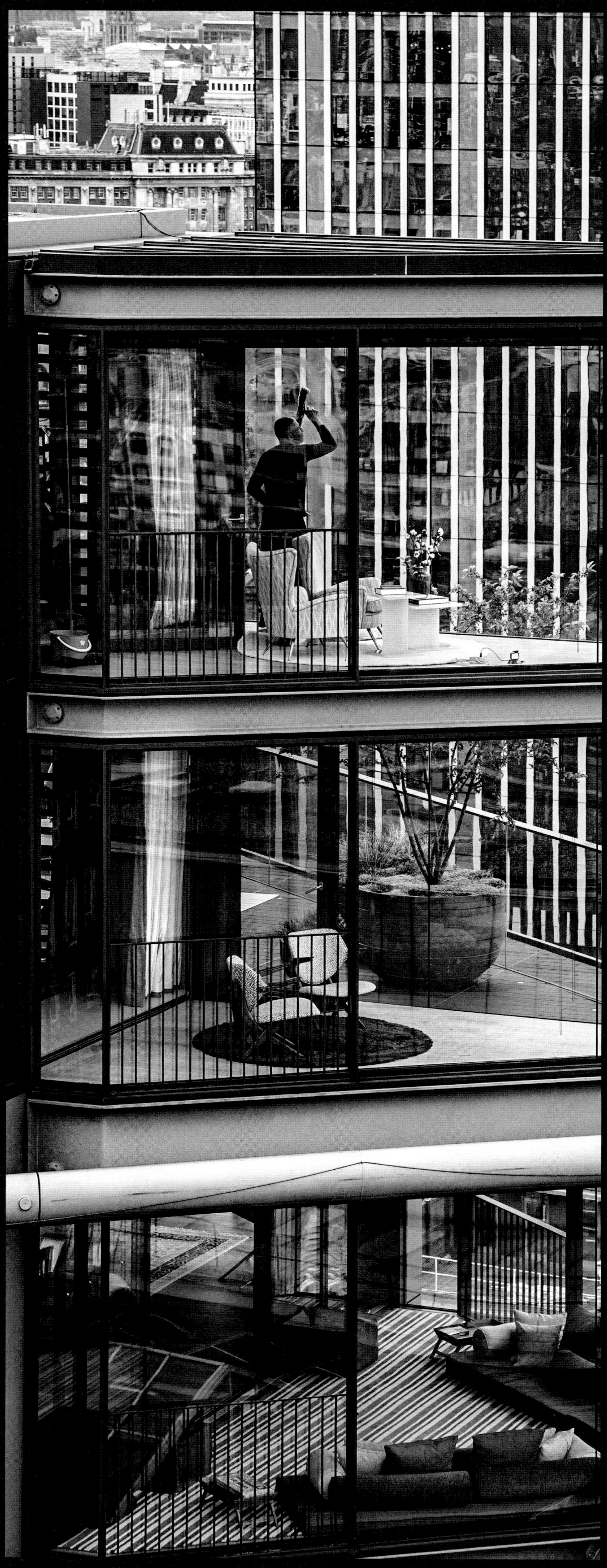

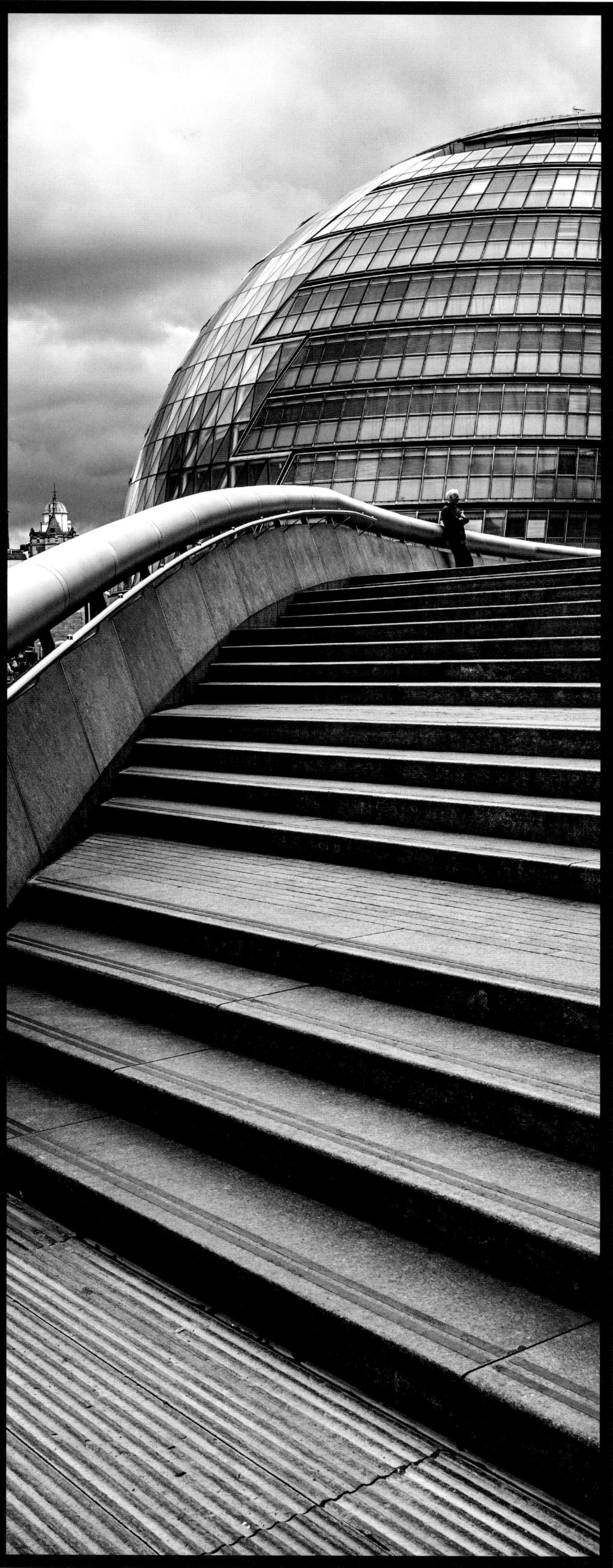

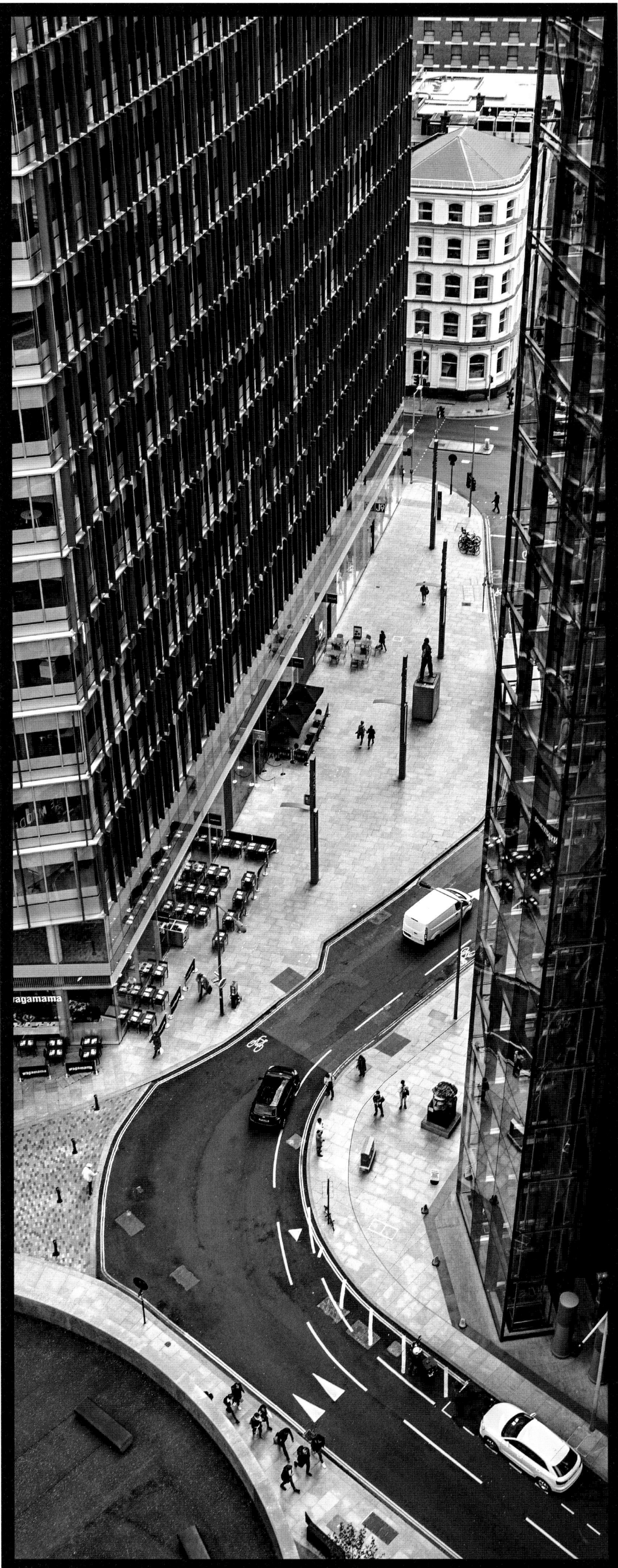

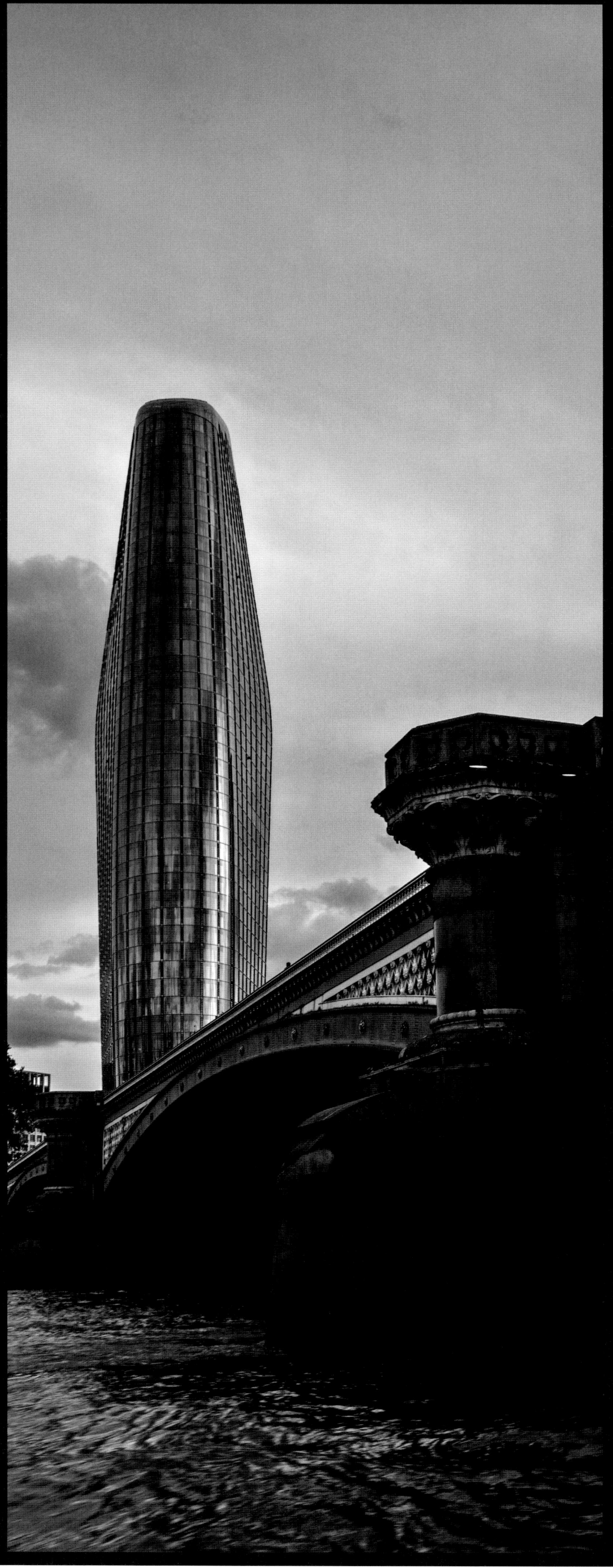

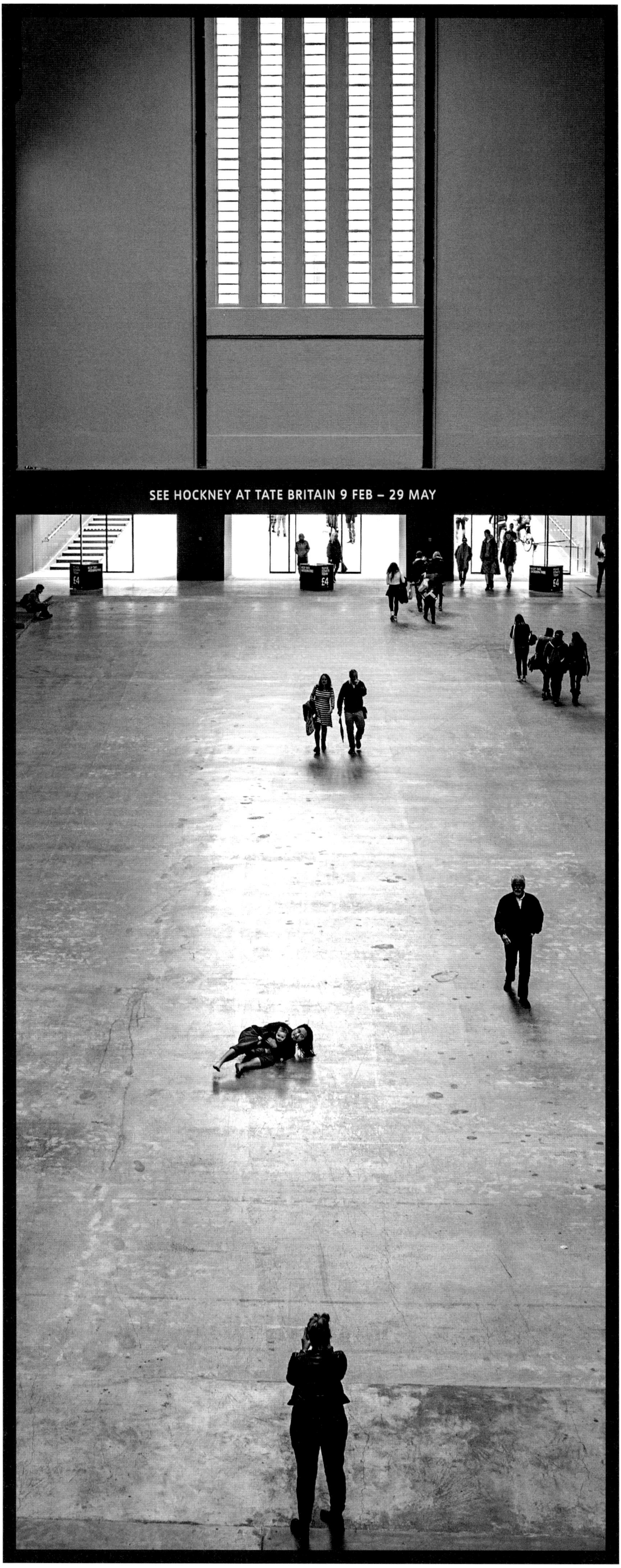

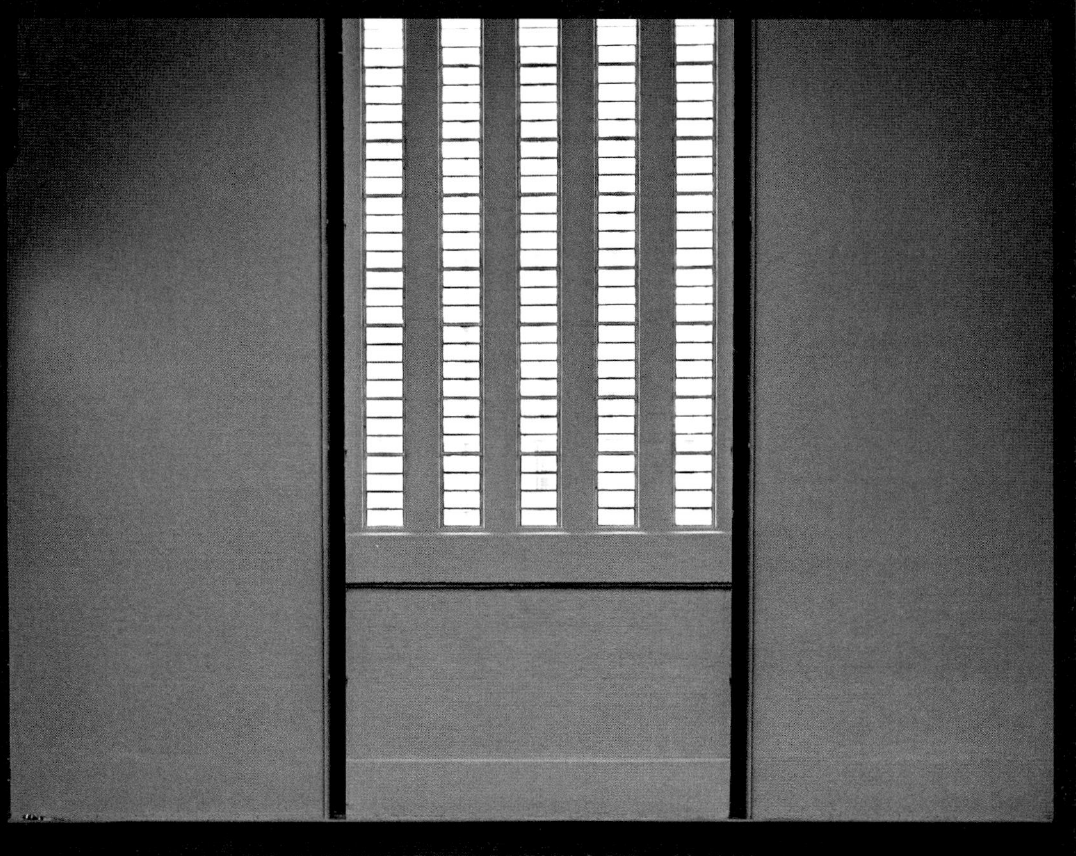

SEE HOCKNEY AT TATE BRITAIN 9 FEB – 29 MAY

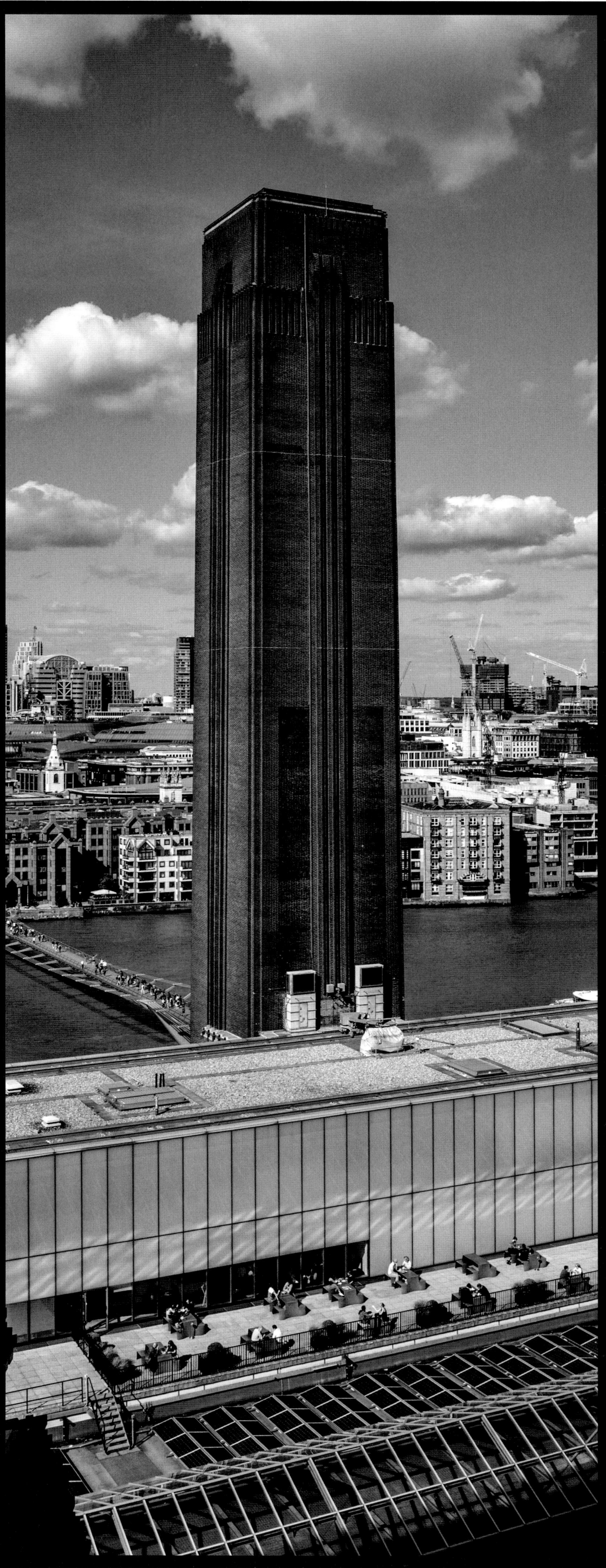

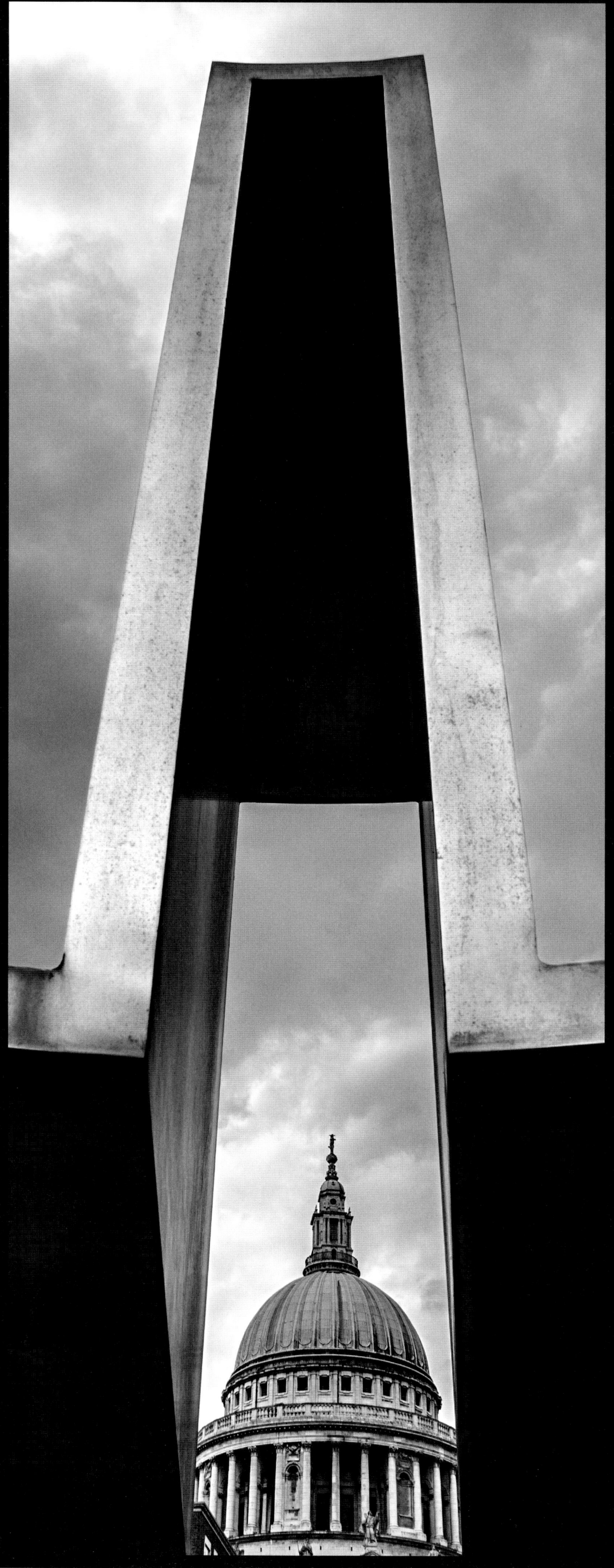

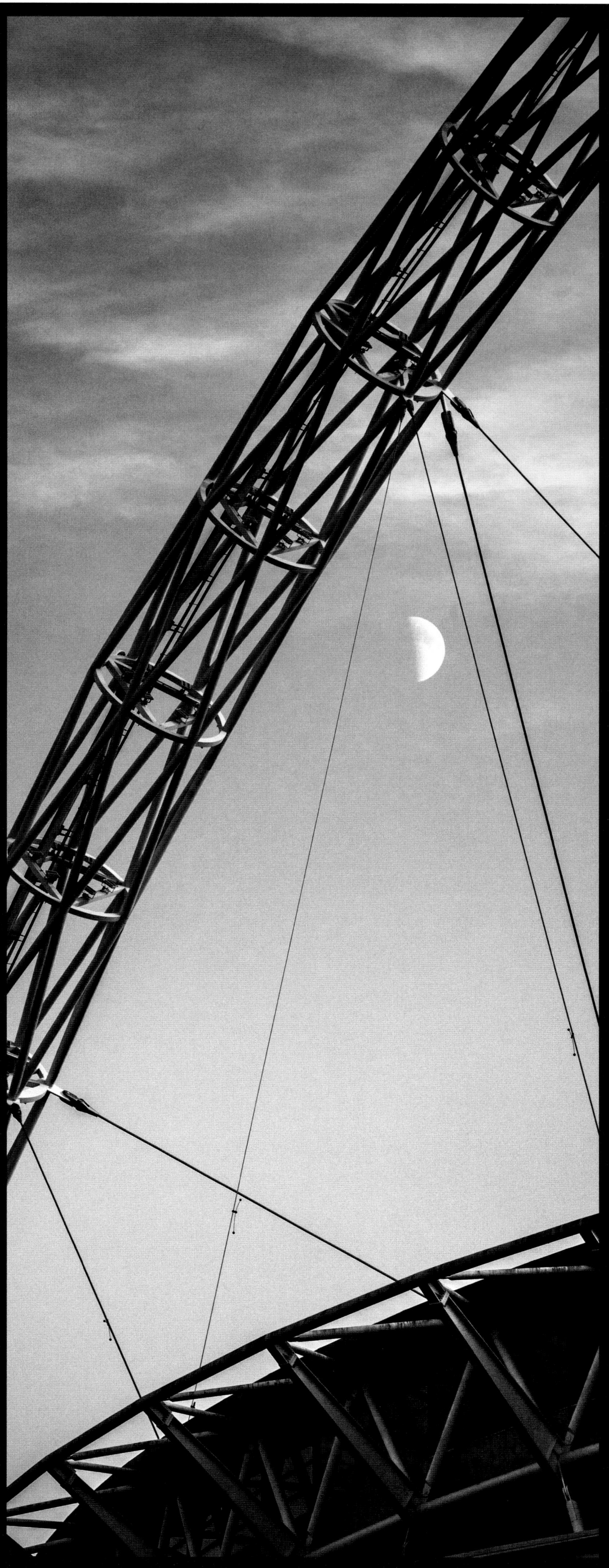

Stamford Bridge / Peter Osgood Statue   124

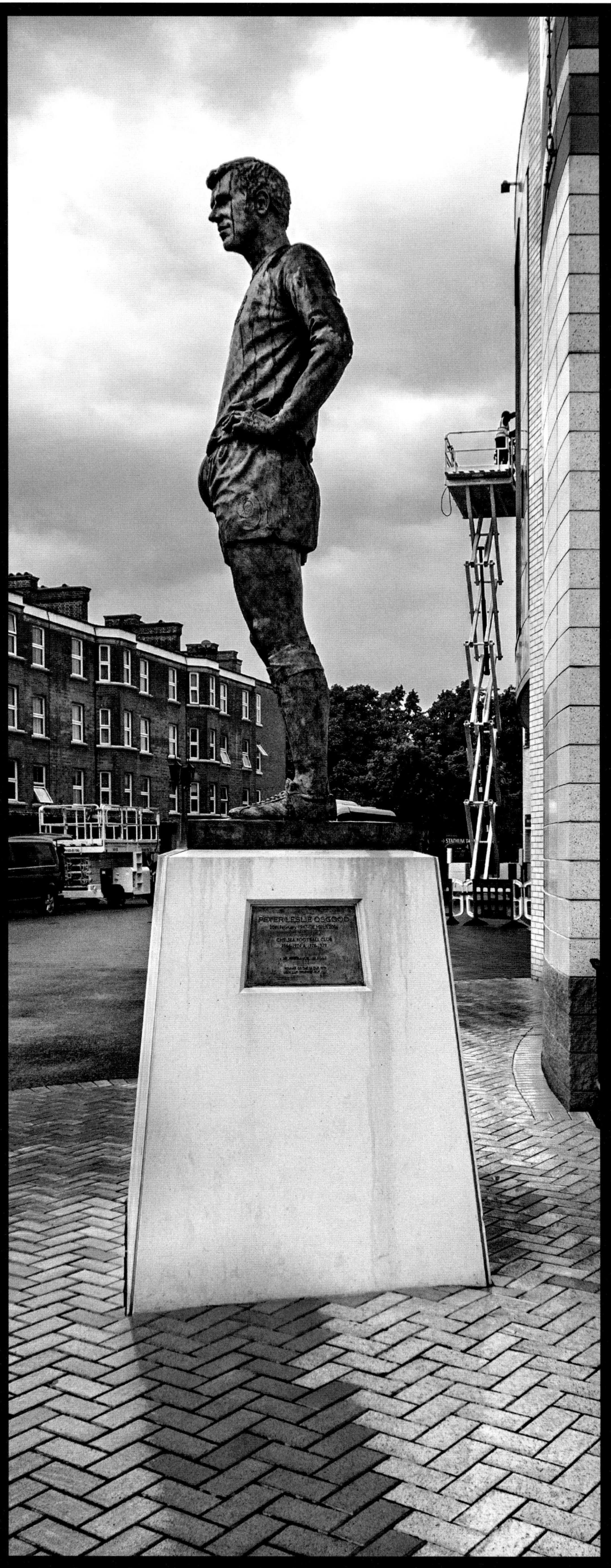
PETER LESLIE OSGOOD
20th February 1947 - 1st March 2006

CHELSEA FOOTBALL CLUB
1964 - 1974 & 1978 - 1979

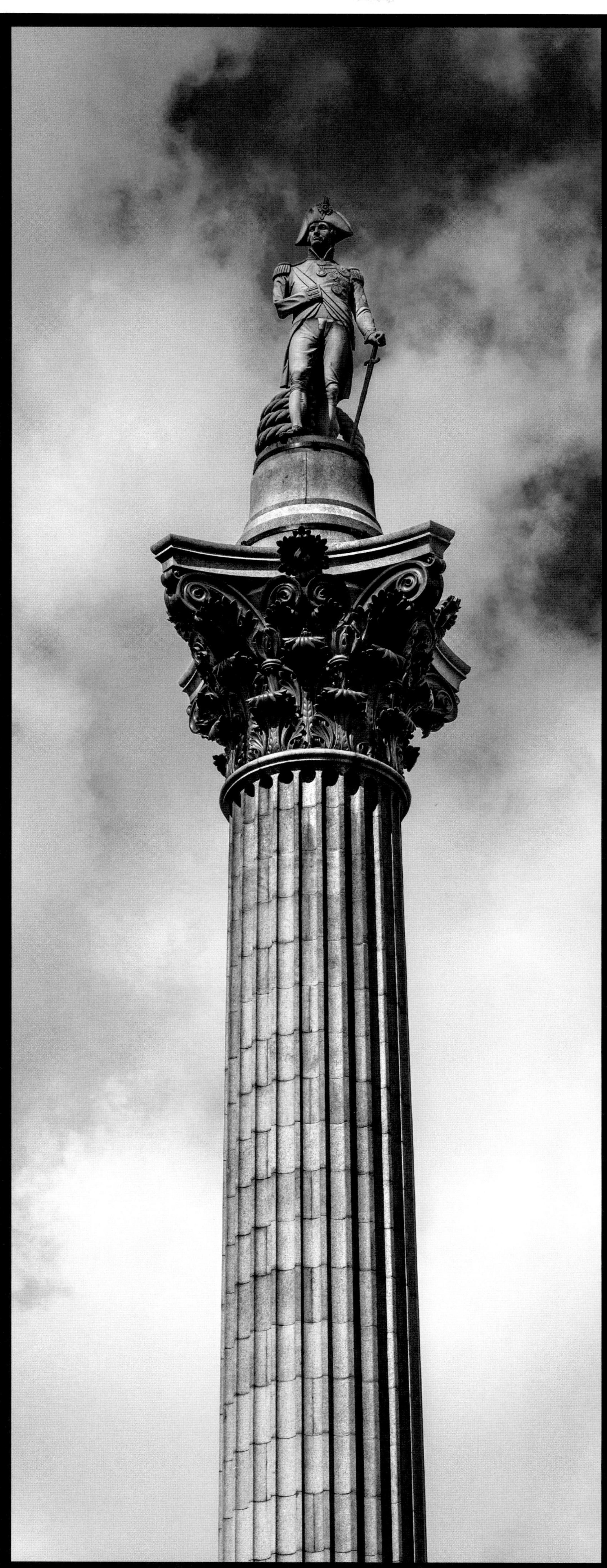

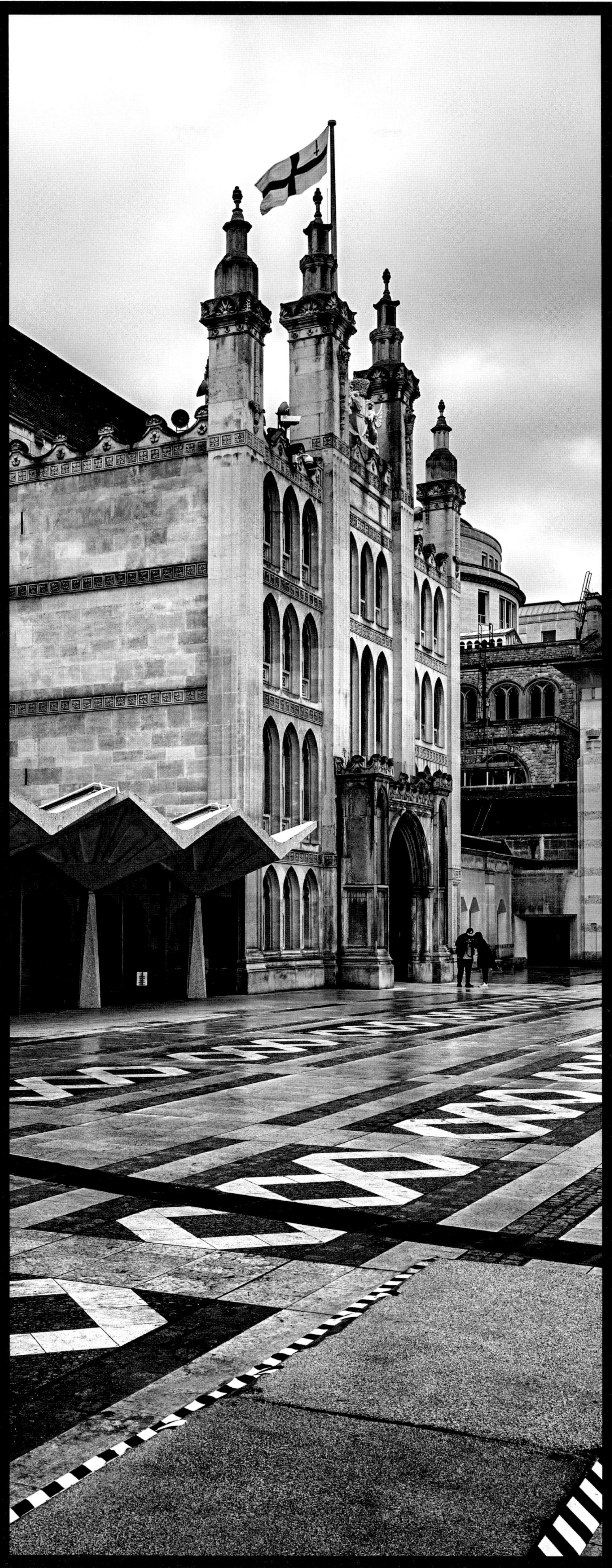

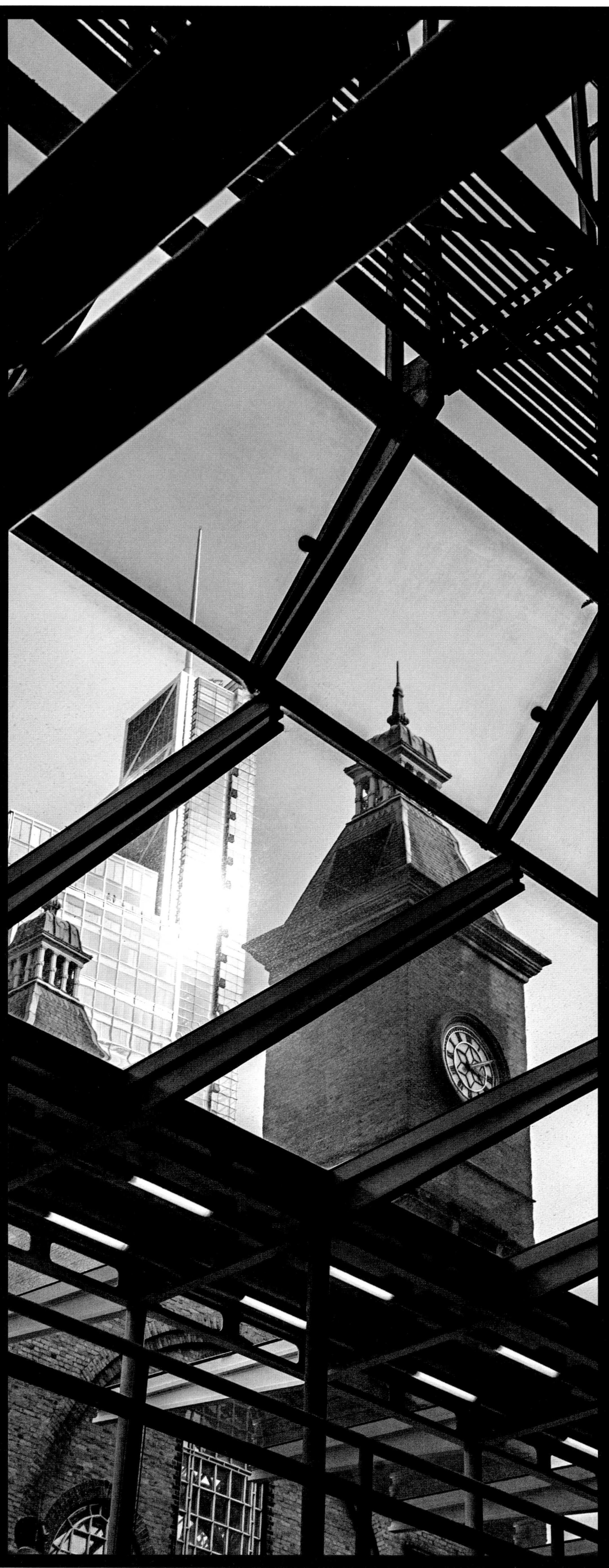

Smithfield Market 132

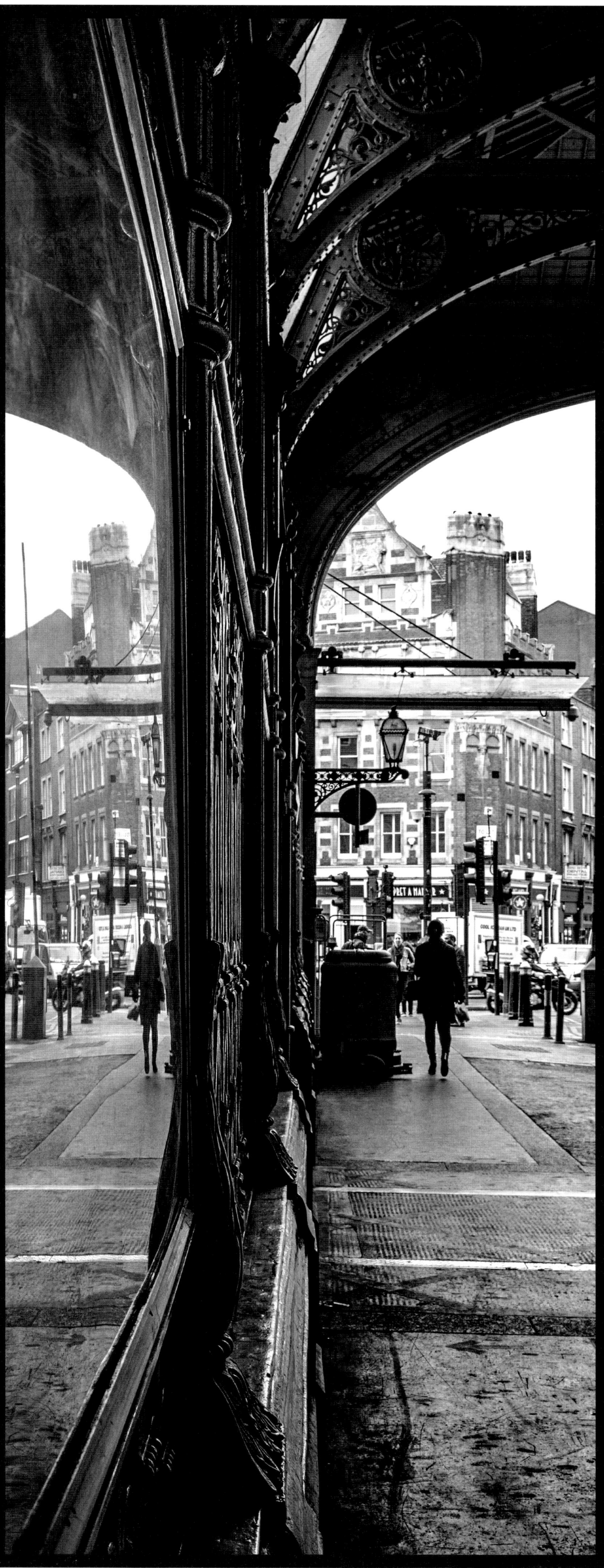

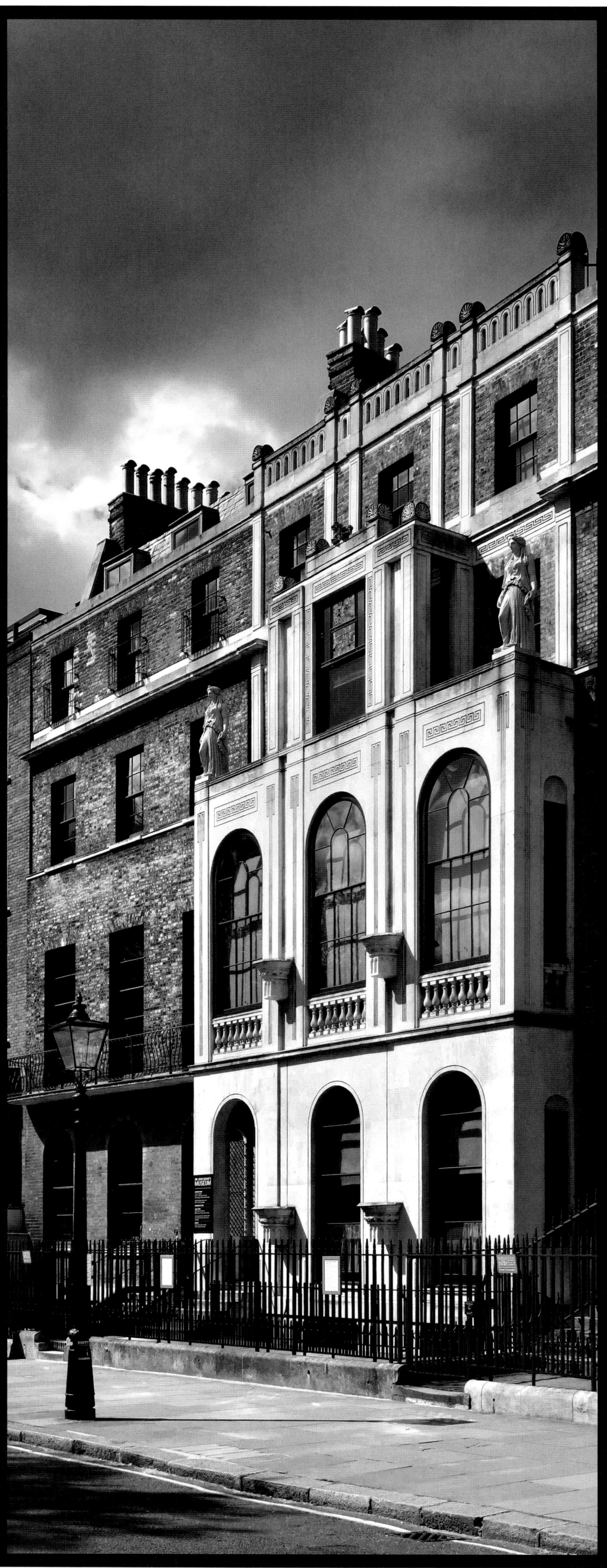

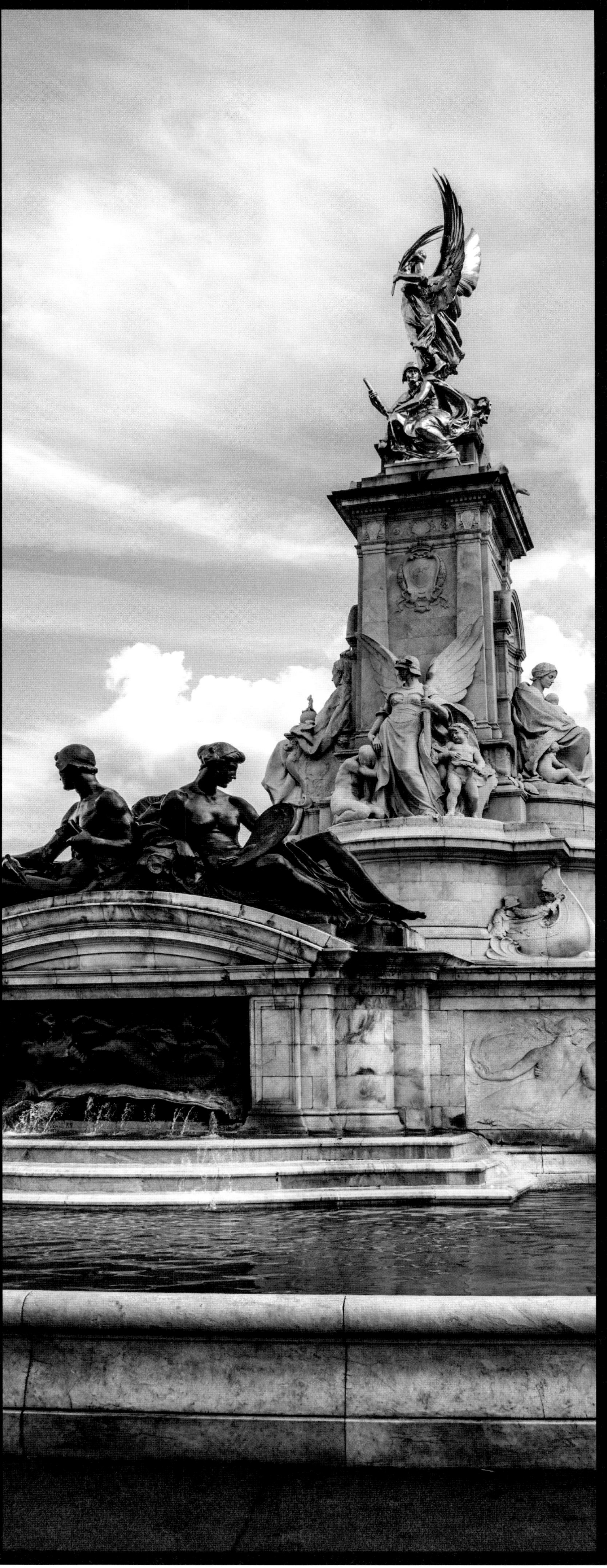

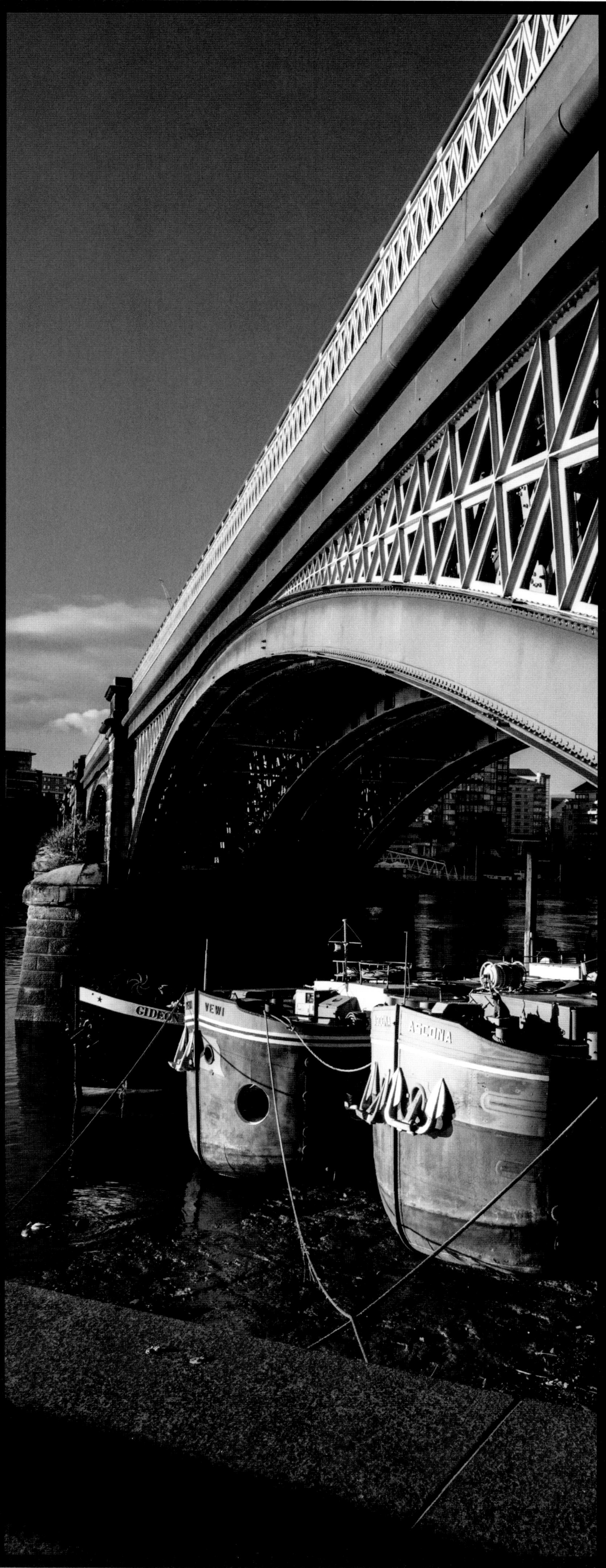

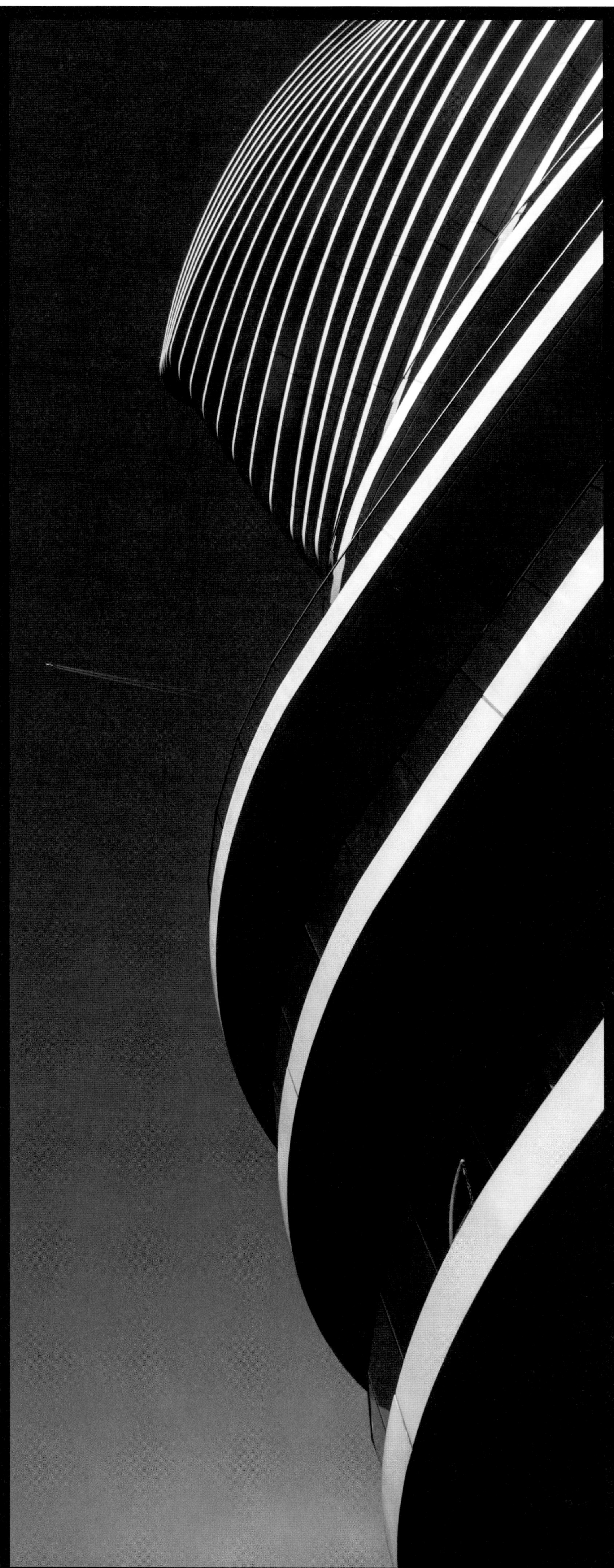

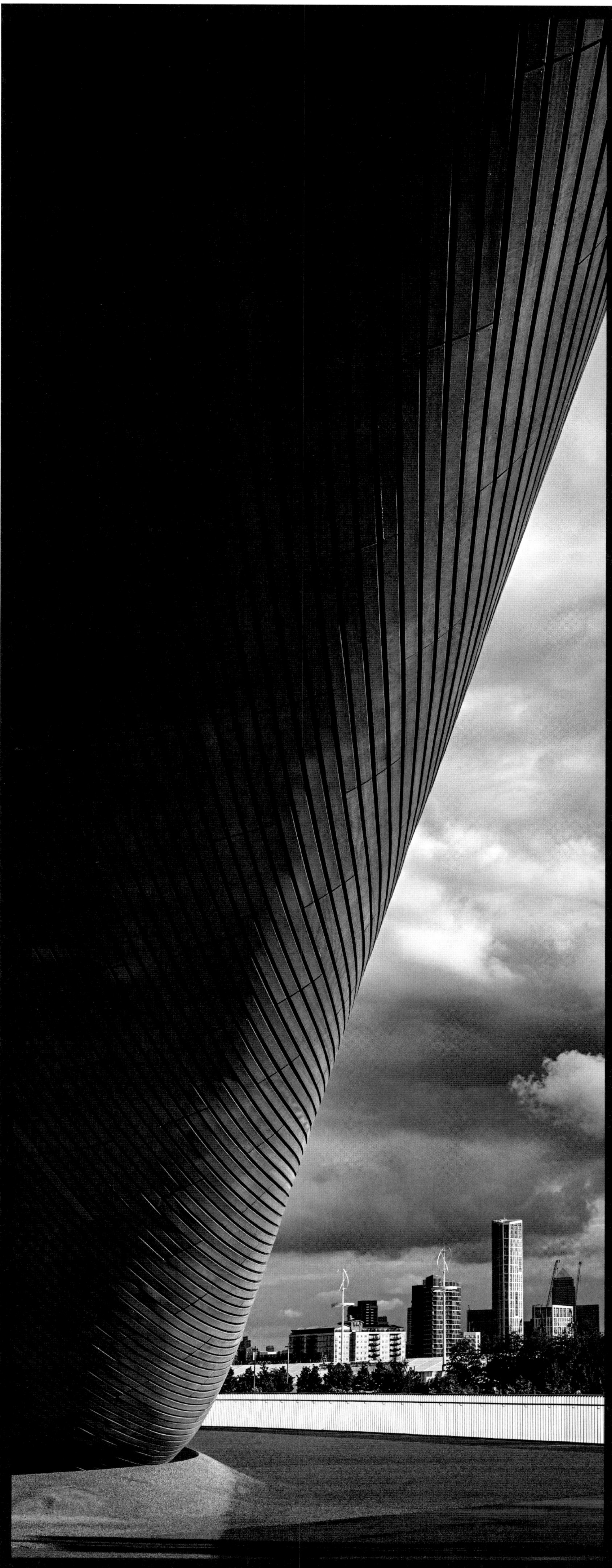

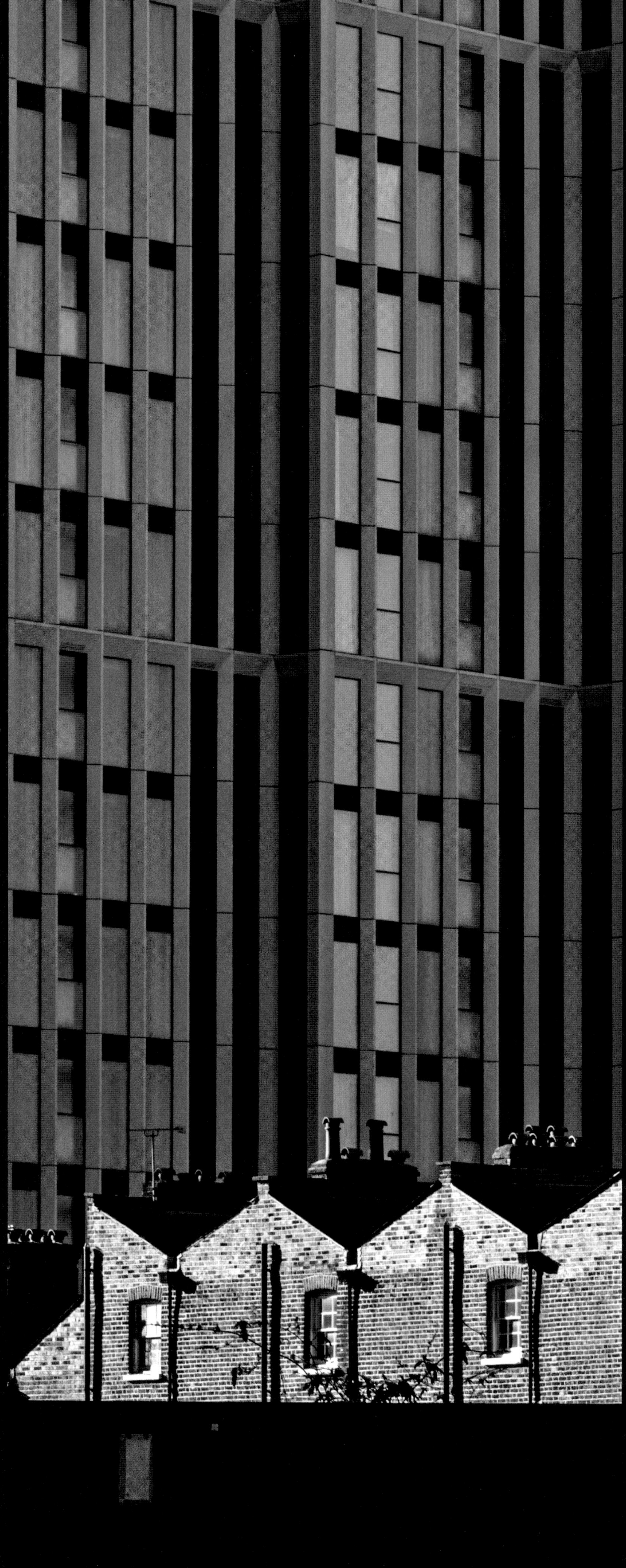

St George Wharf Tower   146

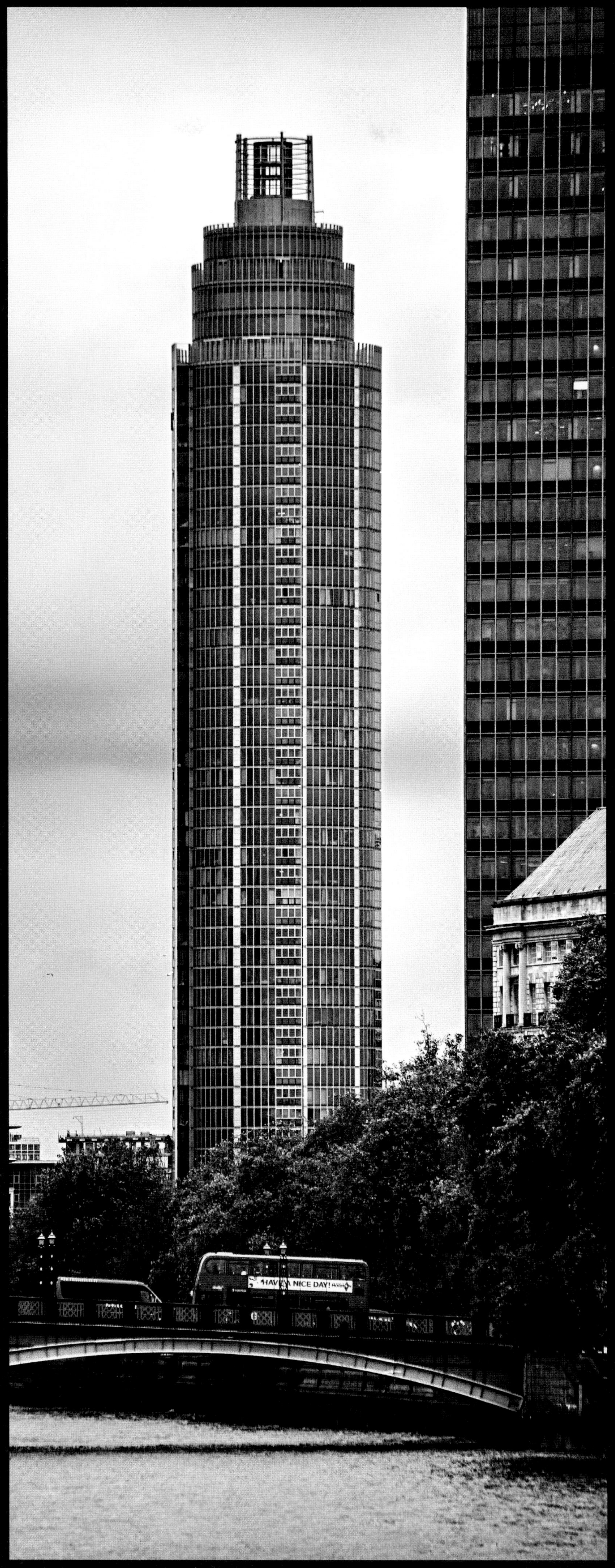

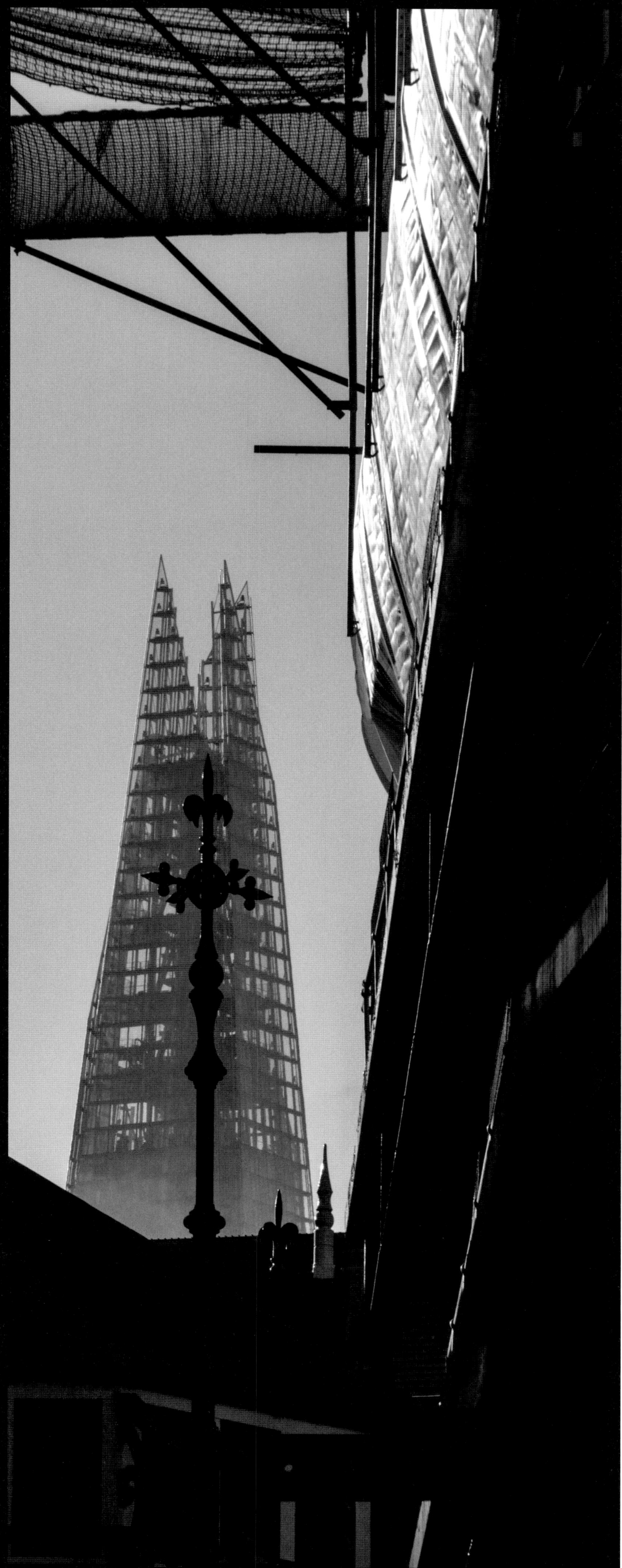

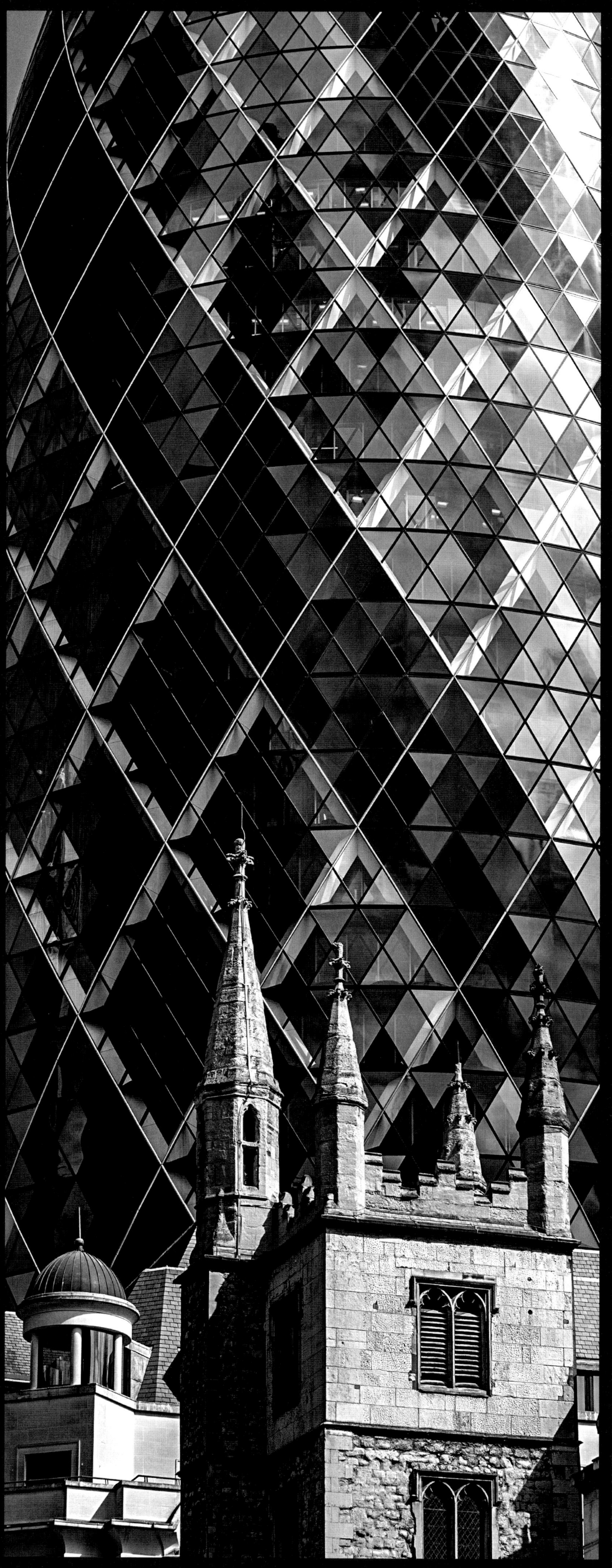

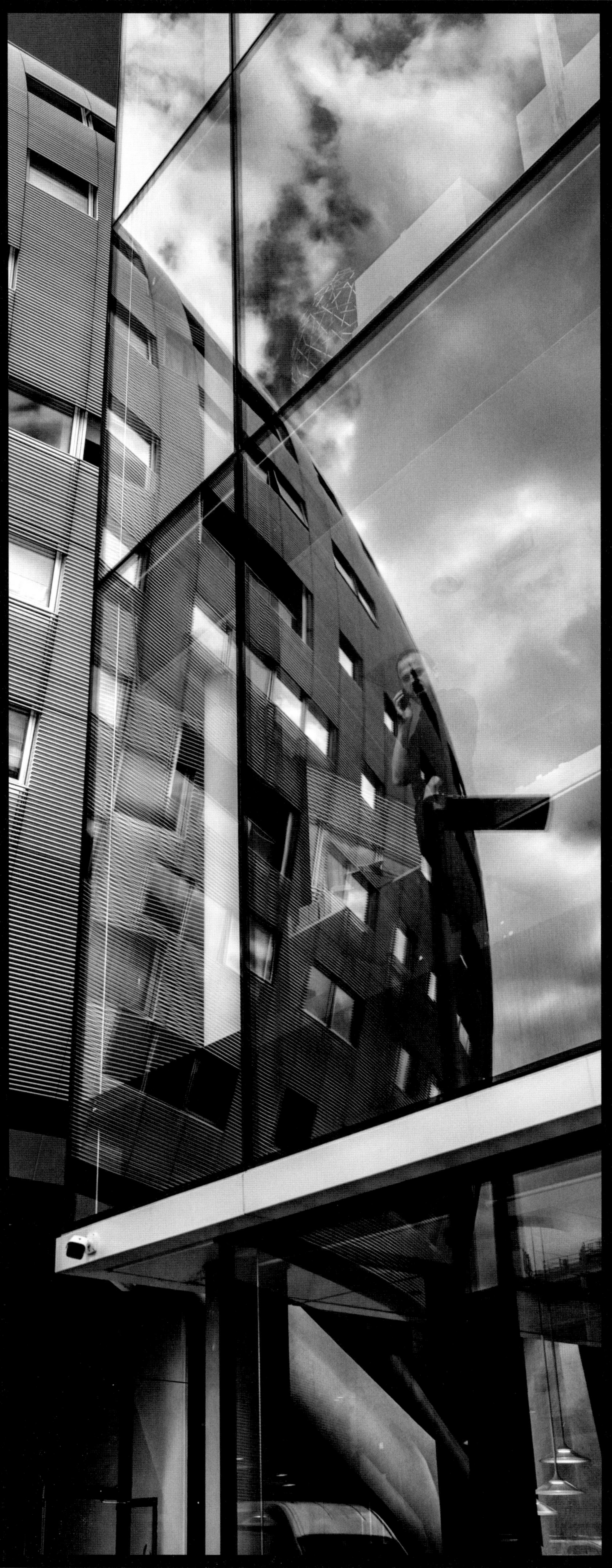

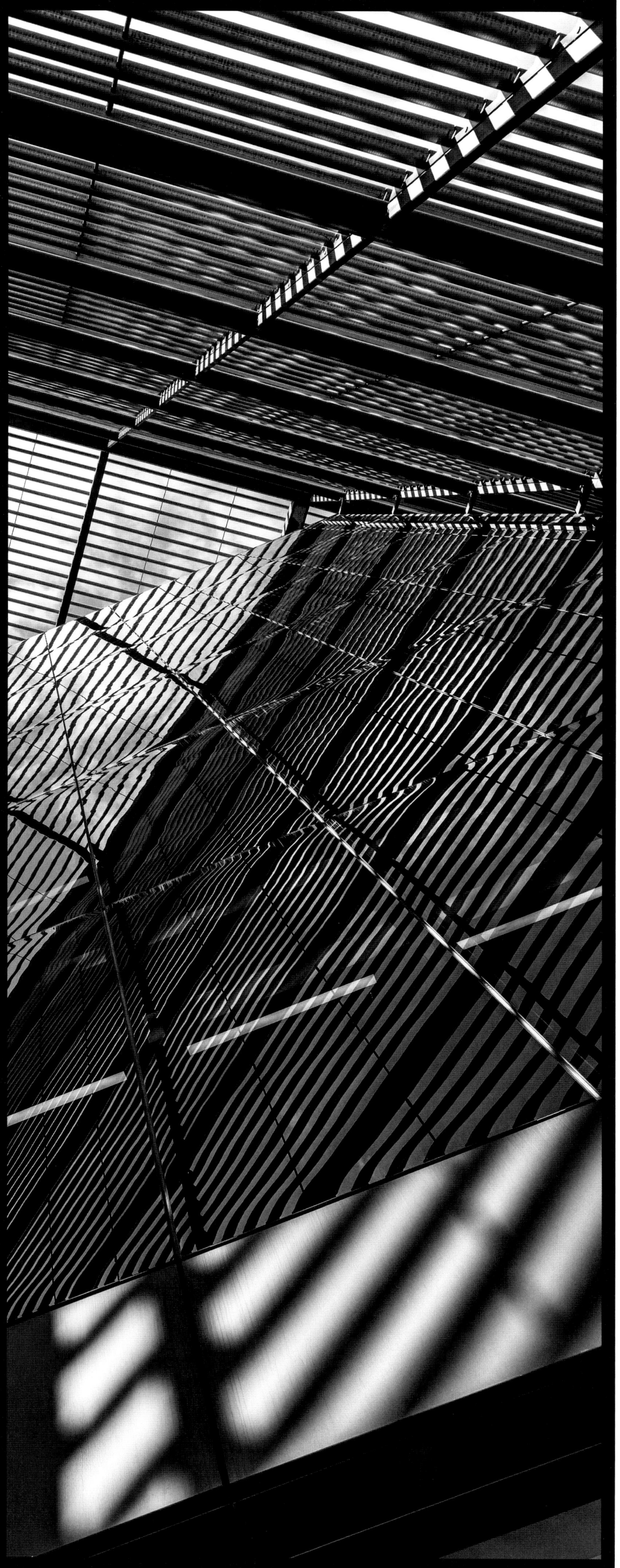

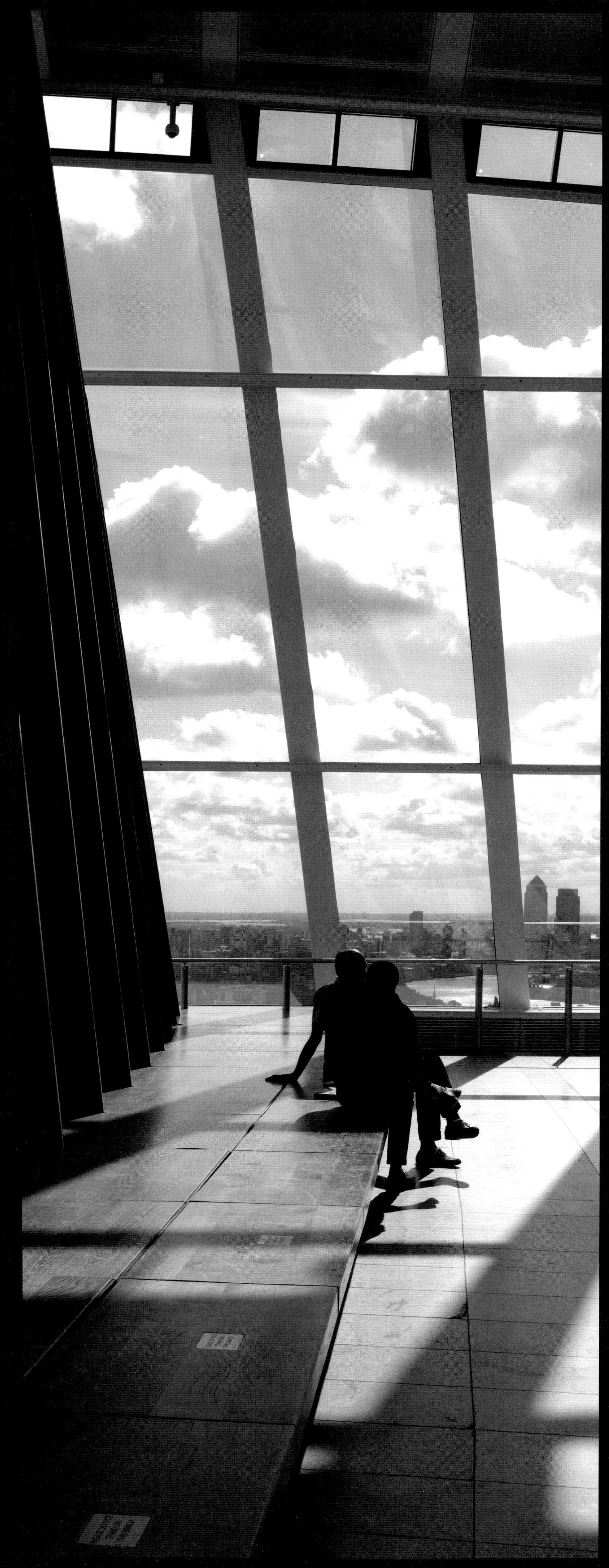

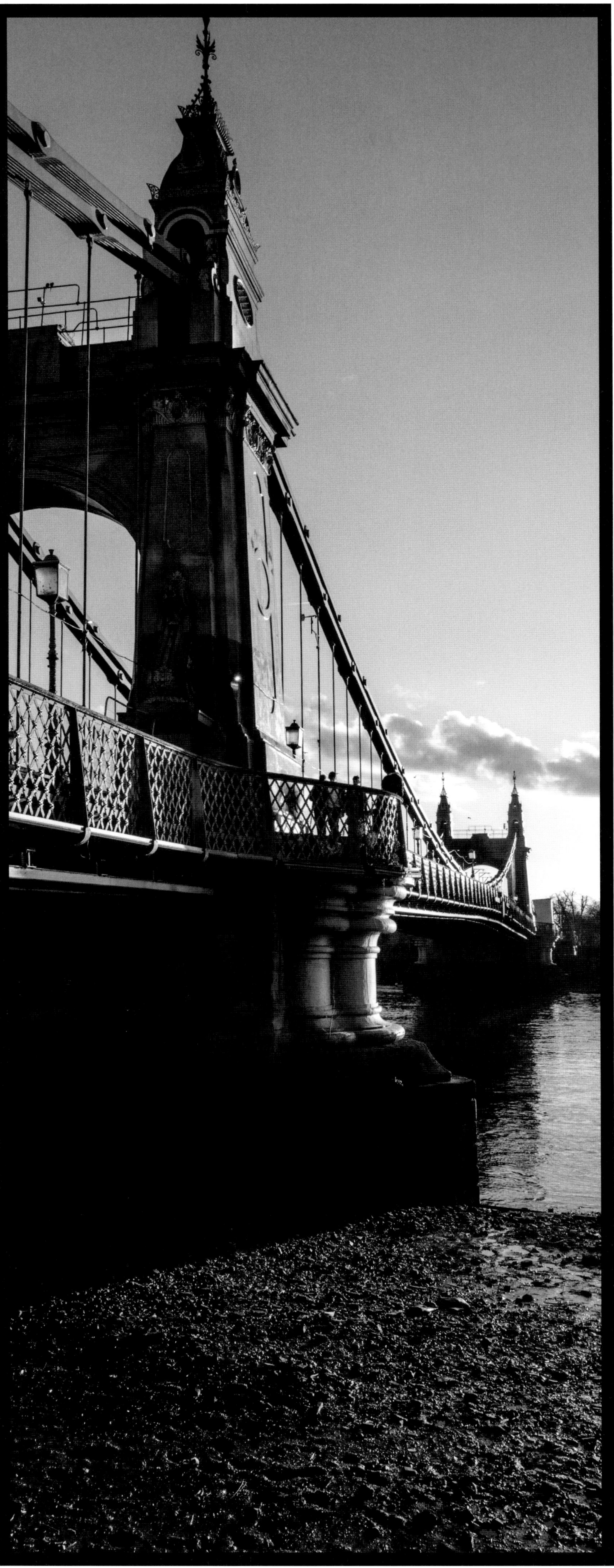

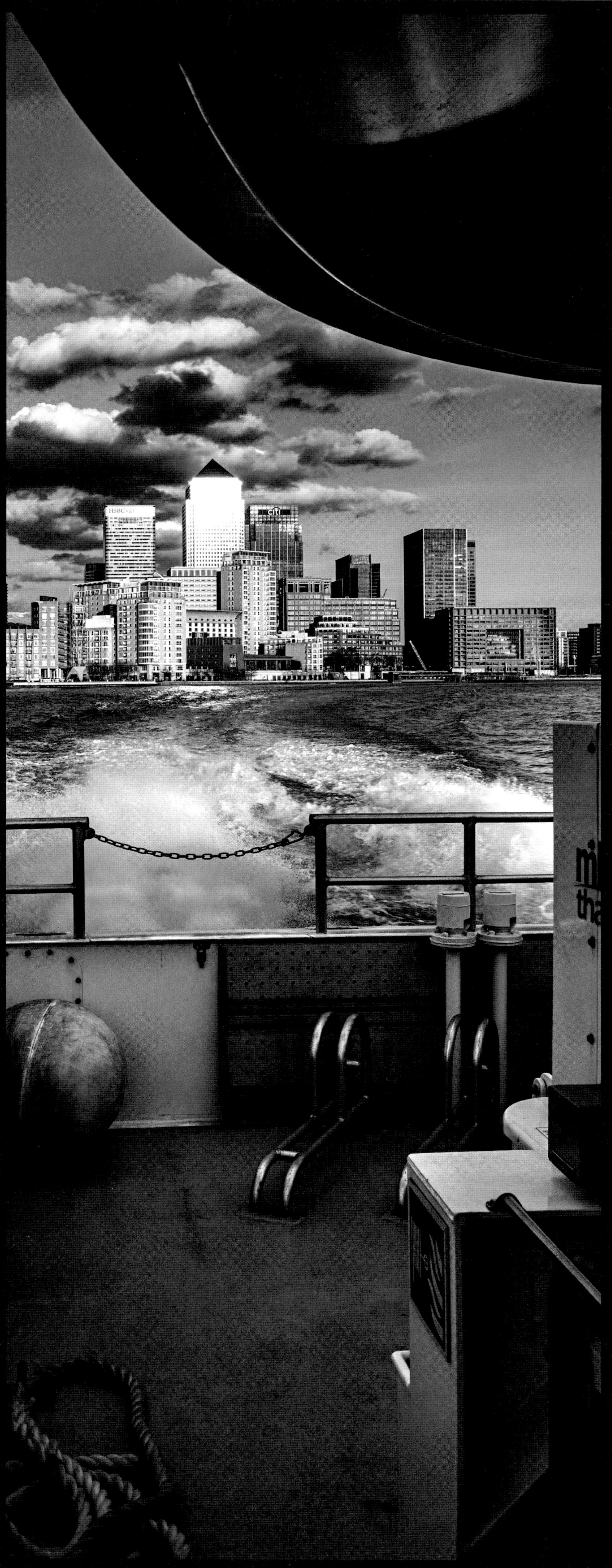

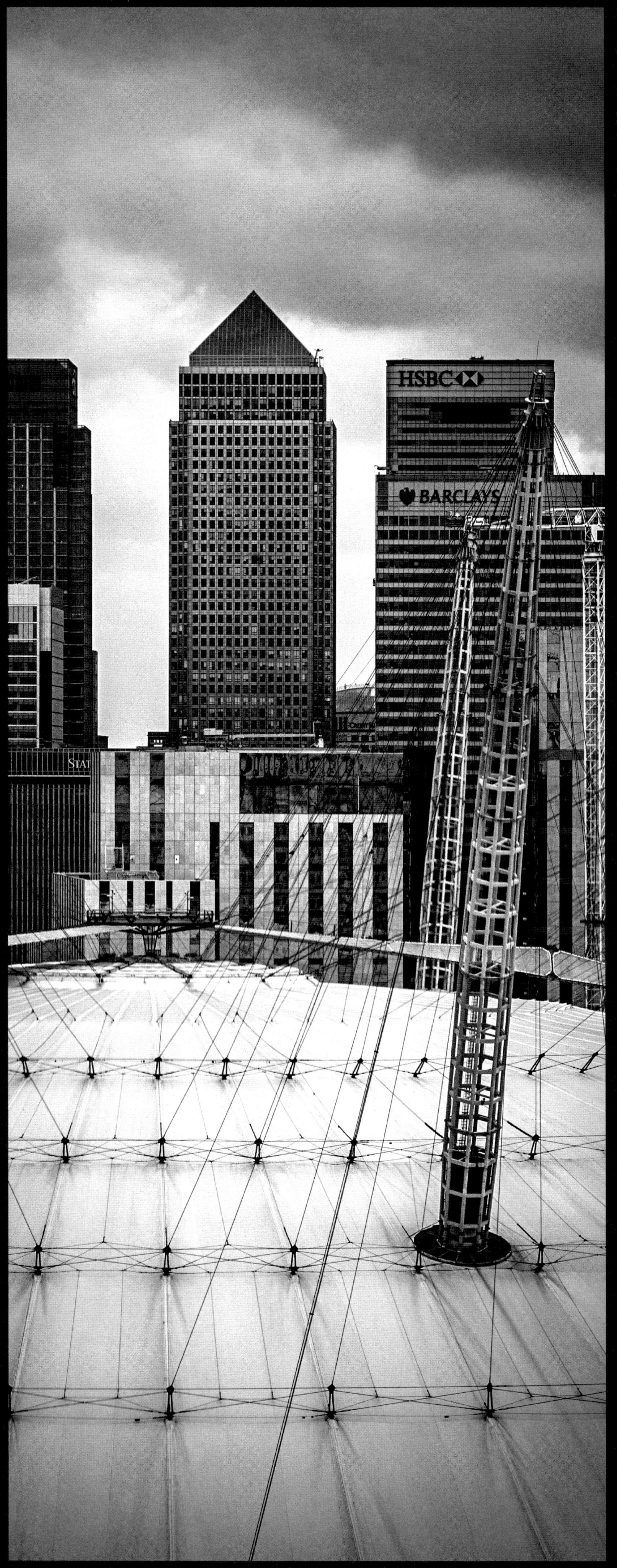

HSBC
BARCLAYS
STAT

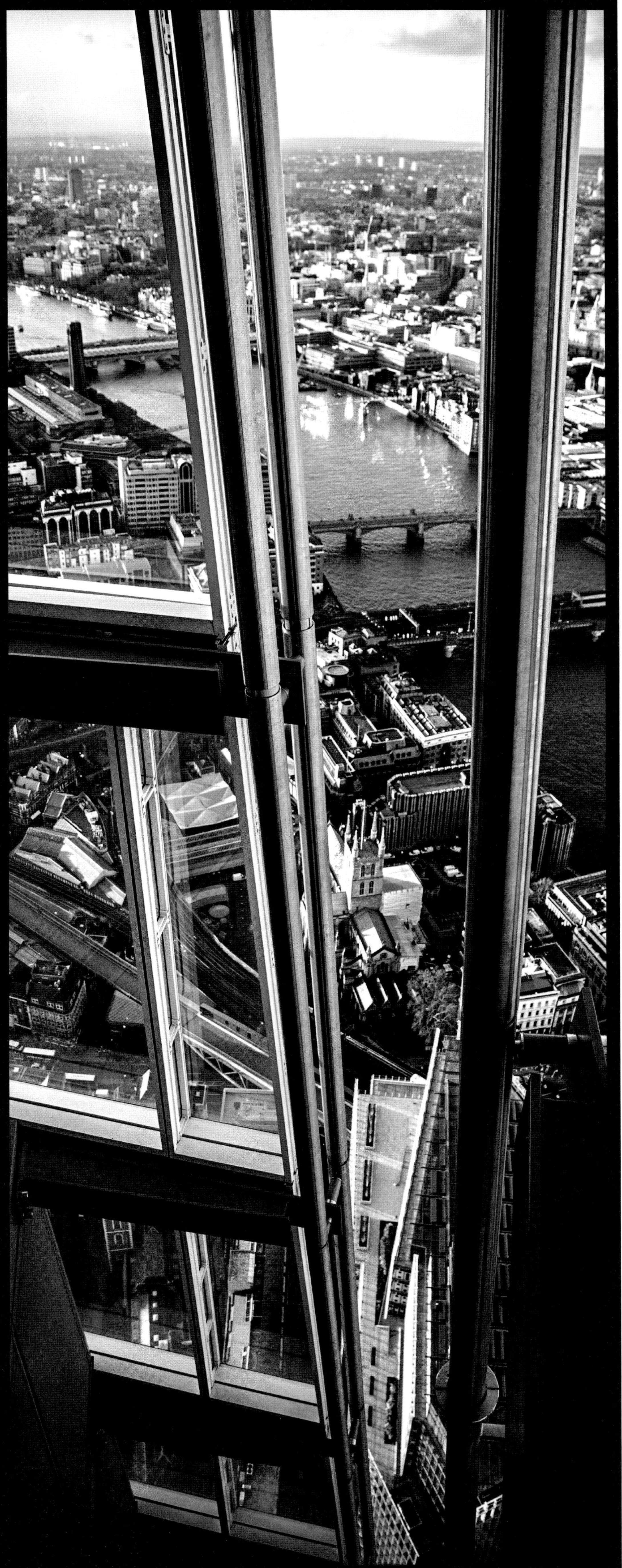

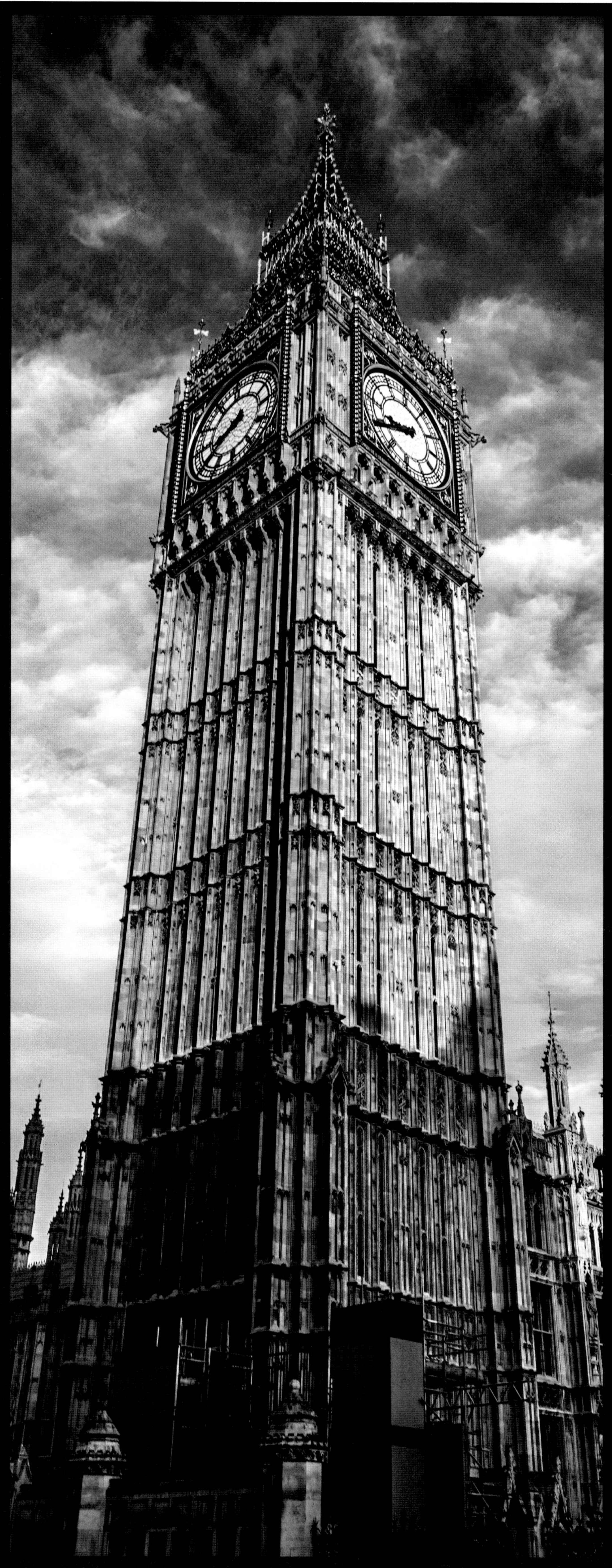

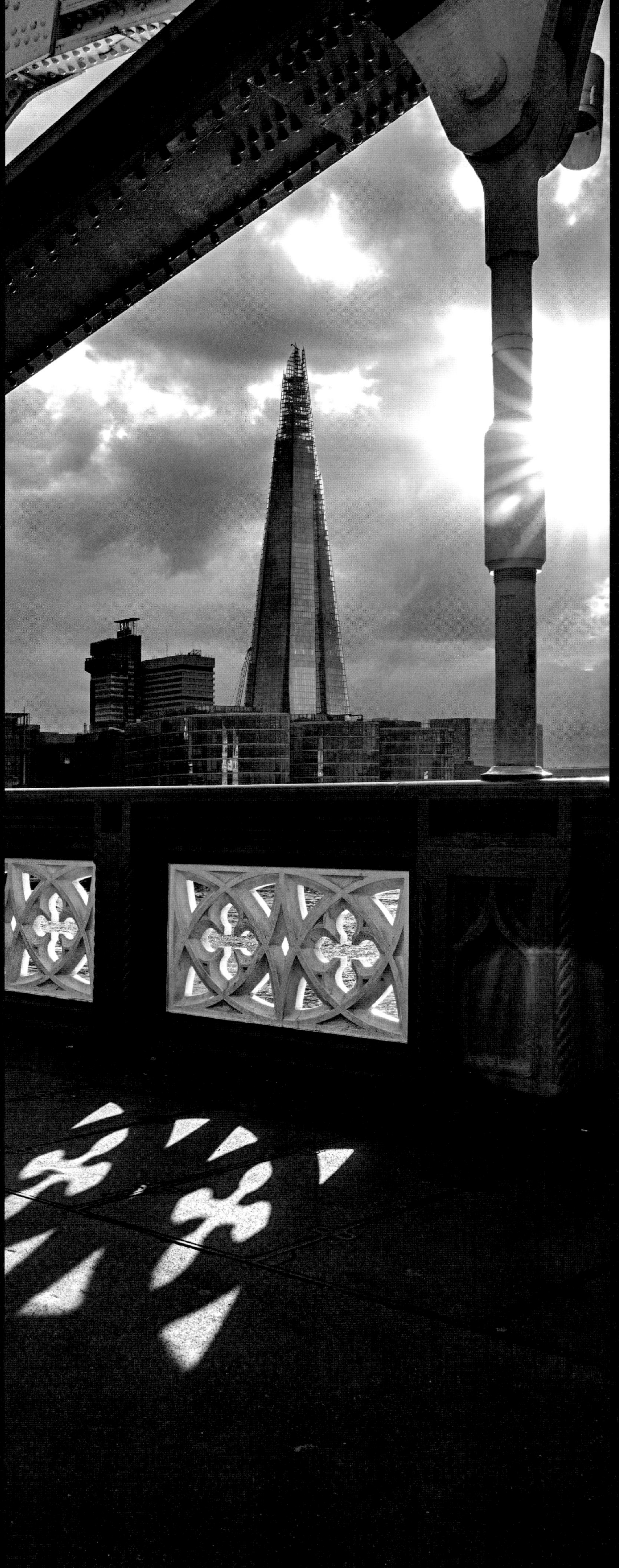

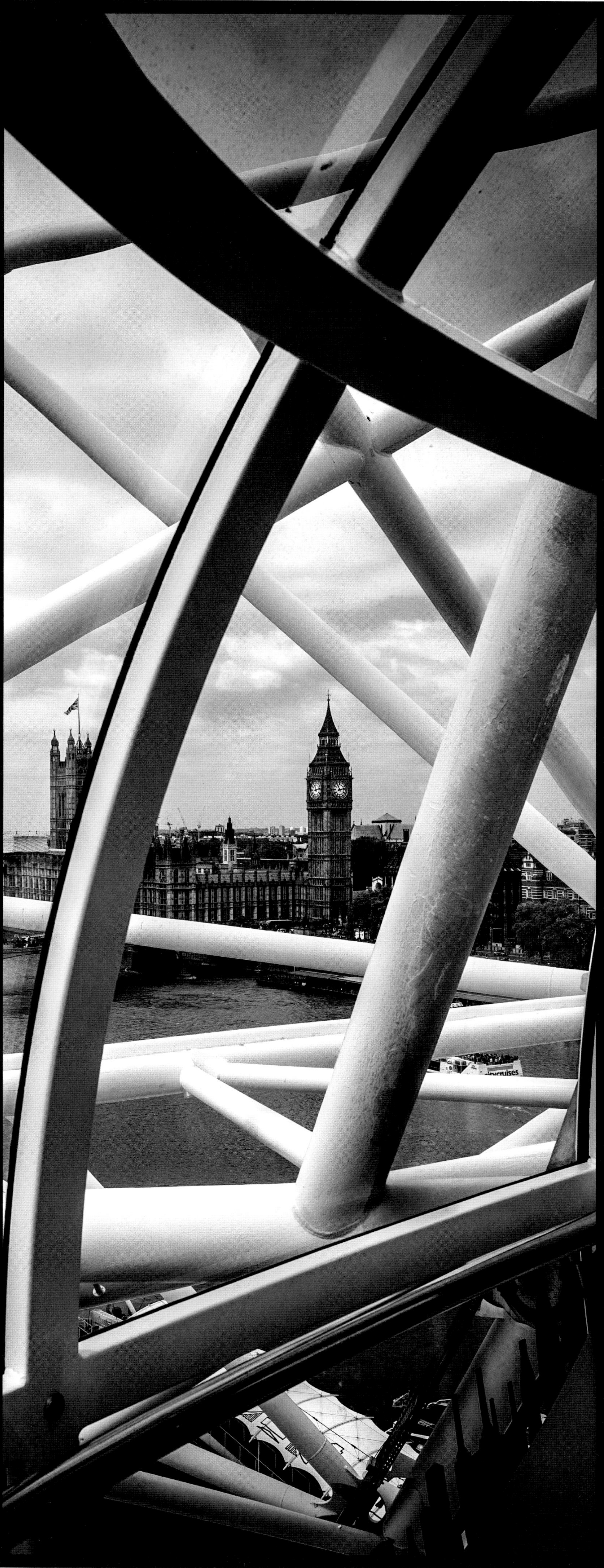

Peter Hamilton   Photo-historian, writer and curator

London is often referred to as "the world's greatest city", although this superlative would inevitably be contested by some other great conurbations. There are certainly bigger and older cities that can challenge it. Nonetheless, since its foundations as a Roman settlement around AD 64 it has survived two millennia of war, plague, fire, social unrest and economic turmoil; as well as the more contemporary challenges from the ever-increasing hordes of tourists, the depredations currently being inflicted by property developers and an uncertain future in the shadow of Brexit.

Some of London's greatness necessarily derives from the fact that it has been the capital of a nation that stood at the head of a great empire, and as a result has benefited greatly and over a long period from the influx of people and commerce from all four corners of the globe – not to mention those closer at hand. Yet London's claim to greatest city status is (naturally enough) unresolved. It is perpetually locked in competition with the other great global cities. New York and Paris are those that will spring most readily to mind, although few would doubt that there are going to be other candidates for this accolade.

Since the late 1830s such great cities have exerted a powerful attraction for photographers of all sorts (as they did beforehand for painters). At present this comes as much from the tourists aiming to capture "selfies" of their trip on their mobile phones as it does from the burgeoning flock of aficionados of "street photography".

Since the 1830s, photography has been uniquely placed to both record and monitor the visual form and evolution of the urban settlements we call London, Paris, New York, etc and as a result has played a vital role in how the city has been seen and more significantly remembered as both idea and reality since the very beginnings of the medium. It is now a commonplace that what the city of the past looked like can best be understood only if there are surviving photographs of it – a "see-change" of huge impact compared to what past generations would have known. There is now a sense in which we can only grasp what it was like to live in a city such as London a century ago, for instance, if we have photographs of the place, its buildings, and its people. This change in visual perceptions was ushered in by the new medium, which right from its beginnings focused on the city. One of L.-M. Daguerrecs very earliest surviving plates are some street views of the Boulevard du Temple in Paris, most probably made in 1838 and thus well before the public announcement of his new process in 1839; whilst on the other side of the English Channel Henry Talbot, his great competitor for the title of inventor of photography, acquired a flat in London's Cecil Street in 1841 with the express intention of using it as a studio and a base from which to photograph the city, but especially because it possessed panoramic river views almost identical to those painted a century earlier by Canaletto.

Six of Talbot's London images survive (including one that shows the construction of Brunel's Hungerford suspension bridge across the Thames, and another of the final stages of the construction of Nelson's column). None, however, are vertical compositions. The only other view of London from the same time and dating from the very beginnings of photography is a portrait format (i.e. upright) daguerreotype plate that shows Wren and Hooke's Monument to the Great Fire built in 1667, a picture that was probably made by Antoine Claudet or Richard Beard around 1842. It may also qualify as the earliest "London Vertical" photograph.

So rapid was progress in the new and untried art of "fixing a shadow" that as early as the mid 1840s it was being exploited in innovative ways to capture the life and architecture of cities: as for example in the half-dozen very rare and remarkably detailed 140-degree panoramic vistas of Paris created around 1845 on curved daguerreotype plates by an artist, Frederick Martens, with a self-invented rotating-lens camera. The painted panorama was a form of art and spectacle that was an invention that was in many ways contemporary with the earliest attempts at the end of the 18th century to create what we now call photography: indeed Daguerre owed his initial fortune and renown to his own version of it (which he called diorama). But it was London itself that had earlier been both host to and subject of the first successful public presentation of the new spectacle: Robert Barker's "panorama" presented at Leicester Square in January 1792 as "a view-at-a-glance of the cities of LONDON and WESTMINSTER, comprehending the three bridges, represented in one PAINTING containing 1749 square feet, which appears as large and in every respect the same as reality." So successful was this that a year later Barker had the means to construct the very first panorama rotunda in Leicester Square, and it soon became a very popular form of public entertainment in the city. Rapidly imitated in

European cities such as Paris until the end of the 19th century, it has reappeared in many forms as public spectacle throughout the world until the present day.

As shown by Martens's 1845 invention (which was a new-technology response to the public fascination with panoramic views evident in the first half of the 19th century) early photographers were swift to imitate their painterly brethren as the new medium developed, making photographic panorama prints of cities and other spectacular vistas of the natural, man-made and social world increasingly popular with the public. But these ultra-wide photographs – whether of a mountain range, a city, the site of a famous battle, or a large group of people – were almost always horizontal images, and although to begin with they were generally montages of prints from overlapping negatives, later they were increasingly made with specialist wide-view and in some cases stereo cameras with one of its two lenses removed leaving a central lens to take a semi-panoramic view on a single plate. Eventually rotating cameras appeared at the end of the 19th century such as the Circut that could encompass an image of up to 360 degrees – a completely circular view. As a result the panoramic photograph has now become most clearly associated in the public mind with something wide, rather than upright (despite the example of Oriental art in which various forms of vertical "panoramas" abound).

Thus it seems remarkable that until the late 1980s, when Horst Hamann began his great and innovative project to photograph one of New York's most visually distinctive aspects – it's characteristic "verticality" – few if any photographers (save perhaps Berenice Abbott in her Changing New York project of the 1930s) had explored this aspect with any consistency and depth in relation to what was by then an increasingly dominant feature of the modern city. Yet lost in the dusty museum there are some relics of the fact that another form of vertical photography had tried to surface. One or two American camera makers of the late 19th-early-20th century produced rare and highly specialised wooden large format "Sky scraper" cameras which resemble a narrow and upright box on which a lens was placed near the top, so it could create an upright rectangular image (or "upright panorama") without converging verticals – no doubt a response to a perceived demand for a camera that could photograph such buildings from street level at the dawn of the "Sky Scraper" age. But few prints made with such cameras seem to have survived, and this aspect of early camera technology now seems largely forgotten.

In searching for some way of bringing a new vision to the great American city where he lived as an aspiring photographer and to a metropolis that had already been endlessly recorded by the great and lesser names of photography since the 19th century, Horst Hamann had begun to experiment with a Linhof Technorama, a large and quite specialized type of camera primarily used by photographers to make wide horizontal "panoramic" photographs on roll film (format 6×17 cm) with an image ratio of 1:3 – a device which from the early 1980s had been popular with advertising photographers to produce letterbox-view images for the multi-sheet billboard posters then in vogue, and also with architectural photographers for landscape-format pictures of buildings.

As a young photographer Hamann had been greatly impressed by the pictures made with a Technorama by the German architect and photographer Klaus Kinold: and eventually managed to acquire one for his own use. He brought it back to America from Germany, but had not been able to make any pictures that satisfied him, and it was only once he started searching for a way of making new types of views of the city in 1991 that he had his light-bulb moment: "I suddenly realised that in New York, all the action is in the sky". By turning the camera onto its side so that it produced upright views in a picture frame whose proportions are roughly 1:3, Hamann thought that he could try to capture in a dynamic way exactly what has made New York so distinctive for the last century or more: the verticality of its built environment, seen from the viewpoint of the typical resident or visitor to the city. "The very last frame I made on one roll of Technorama film was a vertical composition: when I saw it on the contact sheet I thought, wow! that works". From that point on, "think vertical" became his motto, and his first book of his 1991–1995 photographs of "New York Vertical" proved a great success.

Hamann had also broken quite radically with some long-established conventions in architectural photography, particularly one dictating that verticals should always be kept parallel in the image, otherwise the building that is photographed would seem to be distorted (particularly to the architects who are the photographers' main clients). This is really just a visual convention, of course: if one stands on the

pavement and looks up at a tall building then what one sees is that its sides are converging ever closer to each other the higher it rises. The uncorrected camera can only see this. When we are looking upwards our brains merely restore the notion that the sides of the building remain parallel. Because of the demand for verisimilitude in architectural imagery over the last 150 years or so camera designers (and more recently, software programmers) have created ingenious ways of taking photographs looking upwards and, in effect, distorting the images that are created so that the high buildings' verticals do not converge. This involves use of a geometrical rule, known as the Scheimpflug principle – curiously enough, something also deployed in complex eye surgery. Technical cameras and some special "tilt-shift" lenses such as those favoured by architectural photographers for SLR cameras employ this principle in their design so as to allow wide movement of both the film and lens planes to restore parallelism (and software can use the same principle if the image is a digital one). They also require tripods and spirit levels in most cases because the camera must be in a fixed position in order to match both the focal and the lens plane Scheimpflug "swings and tilts" to the subject – and this places a limit on the locations suitable for photography.

Hand-held cameras and Scheimpflug principles thus don't sit easily with each other, and most of the various cameras Hamann has used do not allow this type of image manipulation, precisely because the type of pictures that he wants to make depend on mobility rather than stasis. Thus if a building photographed by him appears to have parallel lines this can only result from how he has sought and found a viewpoint where the structure can be seen like this in real life. New York was, indeed, the site of his apprenticeship in this new form of photography, and the place where he developed his new vision of the city: a project that took more than four years, 400 rolls of film and 1,600 negatives until it could be published. But the photography itself is only the tip of the iceberg in such projects: they involved him in an almost endless process of identifying a viewpoint from the literally millions of possibilities that great metropolises such as New York, (and later Paris and London) can offer, then of getting access to it (officially or otherwise) at times when the light (his chosen quality of daylight) is in the right place and then selecting the framing that will deliver the sort of image he is looking for, and finally of achieving the shot in the best way possible.

For the photographs in "London Vertical", Hamann imposed an intensive and often exhausting shooting schedule on himself, requiring, as he puts it, "walking, walking, walking" throughout the city: sometimes for up to 15 hours at a stretch, during a series of photographic sorties typically lasting up to 4 days at a time. This was combined with careful and detailed research into the architecture of the metropolis – historic, modern and contemporary – to help him make the photographs that would characterise his vision of London in the second decade of the 21st century.

Over the thirty-odd years between photographing for New York Vertical and his study of "London Vertical", Hamann's working tools have also evolved: the big Linhof Technorama was supplanted for his next Paris Vertical project of 1997–2004 by a much smaller Hasselblad X-Pan 35mm film camera, although one using the same panoramic 1:3 image proportions. A decade later for the London book begun in 2015 there would be another technical evolution: and this time for the images reproduced here he has used a digital camera, although one of a very specific and unusual type which is highly optimised to produce his signature black and white images.

The Leica M Monochrom is one of the latest descendants of what has come to be acknowledged as the camera that not only invented the 35mm format, but also came to define "street photography" in the 20th century – the first Leica of 1925. It and its offspring ever since have been the tools of choice of many great artists of the medium, from Aleksandr Rodchenko, Lucia Moholy-Nagy, Henri Cartier-Bresson and Gisèle Freund, to Robert Frank, Mary Ellen Mark and Sebastião Salgado – to name only a very select few. Although the Monochrom is virtually the same size as the very first Leica to be manufactured (and can even use its original Leitz lenses) it is of course a little different inside because the electronics needed for digital capture have replaced the mechanical parts required for exposing 36 frames of perforated cinema film. However, the essence of Leica photography remains the same: there is a viewfinder, a manually focused lens with an aperture ring, and a shutter speed dial. The photographer must still frame the image, focus the lens and decide on the optimum combination of aperture and shutter speed to make his or her photograph.

A quarter century of "thinking vertical" has honed Hamann's photographic perceptions so precisely that he can now "pre-visualise" – as Ansel Adams would have put it – his panoramic compositions. He mentally "composes vertically", identifying the 1:3 ratio of the photograph in his mind's eye even before he starts looking through his Leica's viewfinder.

Apart from offering an artistic interpretation of a contemporary city such as London, a photographer such as Horst Hamann can also play another and vital role in terms of our visual heritage. The photographer is not just the maker of striking images, but also a privileged chronicler of a process of far-reaching change in the urban fabric. As Hamann himself points out, and has so amply demonstrated in his work on New York, Paris and now London, the architecture of the city considered as a visual environment has become increasingly dominated by the vertical dimension. We too as either denizens or visitors have come to adjust to it, and in the case of London have been obliged – as a result – to alter our visual preconceptions of what it represents as a place.

Because it has existed for about 200 years, photography has become key to understanding the visual, cultural and social impacts of long term shifts in the nature, function and form of the city, and in a far more telling way than any other art. This change is only too obvious if one takes the time to compare, for instance, the selection of photographs in "London Vertical" with those in a recent English Heritage publication, Panoramas of Lost London. The latter records the buildings and cityscape lost to destruction in London for various reasons but mainly from fire, war, dereliction and urban renewal, over the period 1870–1945. Although none are in reality truly "panoramic" photographs, the use of details enlarged from the mainly very large format negatives and prints archived by the London County Council from the 1880s onwards portray a metropolis in which the vertically dominant buildings – mainly churches, cathedrals and monuments such Nelson's column or the Monument itself – stand out in all their pomp from the dominant mass of impressive but essentially horizontally grand but also in many cases modest buildings that formed the London of the late 19th century and the first half of the 20th century.

Hamann's recent photographs of London record, naturally enough, certain of those iconic vertical buildings that a Londoner of 1918 would still recognise a century later, but if one excludes those pictures that include the same building more than once as part of a composition, only a handful of those 17th to 19th century buildings remain visible as characteristic features of the contemporary London cityscape, and even these are in many cases dwarfed by far more recent and mostly 21st century structures. Few of these new buildings are uncontroversial, either in architectural or planning terms. Many have been associated in the public mind with social, political and economic changes that are widely considered to be divisive and inegalitarian. In building terms one obvious example is "Sky Garden" in Fenchurch Street, the so-called "Walkie-Talkie", whose wider shape at its top reflects the fact that in London the rents that can be charged increase greatly the higher the floor being inhabited. The Guardian newspaper commented that: "As a literal diagram of developers' greed, it provides the painful proof that form follows not function but finance. An aberration of the planning system, the building stands alone outside the planned City cluster, like the school bully expelled from the classroom, poking its unwelcome bulk into the skyline from almost every possible vista."

Whatever view one takes of the "verticalisation" of London over the last few decades, it would be instructive perhaps to contrast London with Paris intra muros. For despite the myriad and often dismal tower blocks of the banlieue that ring the périphérique, only one skyscraper has ever been allowed to blight what still remains of the Parisian cityscape so hauntingly captured by Charles Marville (another predecessor of Hamann) at the height of Haussmann's renovation in the 1860s. This building was the Tour Montparnasse: a structure so controversial and so widely disliked that two years after its completion in 1973 the construction of buildings over seven stories high in the city centre was banned. Some might argue it is a shame a similar decision was never taken by the mayor of London.

Notwithstanding the numerous controversies over the development of high buildings in London since the 1960s, it is surprising to note that there appear to have been very few renowned photobooks about this city made by leading photographers that concentrate mainly on its built form. Even classics of the photobook genre concerned with London and made by "auteur" photographers, as for example Charmes de Londres by Izis with a text by Jacques Prévert (Guilde du Livre, 1952: also

published in an English language edition), are comparatively few and far between and rarely concentrate primarily on the built environment, especially by comparison with those on Paris and New York, and none to my knowledge have offered vertical panoramic photographs until now.

Apart from the work of Marville although it was never published in book form during his lifetime, possibly the nearest equivalent to Hamann's oeuvre is in fact another book of panorama photographs, Josef Sudek's very rare and greatly sought after 1956 photogravure publication about Prague, Praha panoramaticka. Although mainly composed of horizontal panoramic pictures, it also contains some vertical photographs. It is perhaps unsurprising to learn that the work of the Prague master is greatly admired by Hamann who demonstrates a comparable feeling for the balance of light, space and form in his images. And I would humbly if confidently predict that the quality of vision and distinctiveness of his photographs in "London Vertical" will make it a book that will be as keenly sought after in years to come as that of Hamann's illustrious Czech predecessor.

177

Peter Hamilton   **Fotohistoriker, Autor und Kurator**

London wird oft als „die größte Stadt der Welt" bezeichnet und das, obwohl dieser Superlativ zwangsläufig von einigen anderen großen Ballungsräumen angefochten wird. Es gibt sicherlich größere und ältere Städte, die diesen Titel für sich beanspruchen könnten. Dennoch überstand London seit der Gründung als römische Siedlung um 64 n. Chr. zwei Jahrtausende Krieg, Pest, Feuer, soziale Unruhen und wirtschaftliche Turbulenzen und wird auch die moderneren Herausforderungen wie die immer größer werdenden Touristenströme, die von Projektentwicklern verursachten Verwüstungen und eine ungewisse Zukunft im Schatten des Brexits überstehen.

Ein Teil von Londons Größe resultiert sicherlich aus der Tatsache, dass sie die Hauptstadt einer Nation ist, die an der Spitze eines großen Imperiums stand, und dadurch wesentlich und über eine lange Zeit durch die Menschen und den Handel aus allen Teilen der Welt – ganz zu schweigen von der einheimischen Bevölkerung – profitierte. Doch Londons Anspruch, die größte Stadt der Welt zu sein ist (selbstverständlich) ungeklärt und befindet sich im ständigen Wettbewerb mit anderen Weltstädten. New York und Paris kommen einem am ehesten in den Sinn, obwohl nur wenige daran zweifeln, dass es durchaus weitere Kandidaten für diese Auszeichnung gibt.

Wie zuvor für Maler üben solche Großstädte seit Ende 1830 eine starke Anziehungskraft auf Fotografen aller Art aus. Aktuell tragen sowohl die Touristen, die auf ihren Reisen Selfies auf dem Handy festhalten, als auch die aufkeimende Liebe zur Straßenfotografie zu dieser Attraktivität bei (siehe auch Stadt- oder urbane Fotografie aller Art.

Seit 1830 ist die Fotografie ein ideales Medium, um sowohl die visuelle Form als auch die Entwicklung der städtebaulichen Siedlungen (wie London, Paris, New York usw.) zu dokumentieren und zu beobachten. Sie spielt eine entscheidende Rolle, wie die Stadt gesehen wird und noch wichtiger, wie sie in Erinnerung bleibt. Man ist sich heute darüber einig, dass die Vergangenheit einer Stadt besser zu verstehen ist, wenn Fotografien erhalten sind. Nur so werden Veränderungen über Generationen hinweg sichtbar. Aufnahmen beispielsweise von Plätzen, ihren Gebäuden und ihren Menschen vermitteln uns ein Gefühl, wie es war, in einer Stadt wie London vor hundert Jahren zu leben.

Diese Veränderung der visuellen Wahrnehmung wurde durch das neue Medium eingeleitet, das sich von Anfang an auf die Städte konzentrierte. Eine der frühesten von L. M. Daguerres erhaltenen Fotoplatten zeigt einige Straßenansichten des Boulevard du Temple in Paris, höchstwahrscheinlich 1838 aufgenommen, und damit lange vor der offiziellen Vorstellung seiner neuen Technik im Jahre 1839. Gleichzeitig erwarb auf der anderen Seite des Ärmelkanals Henry Talbot, sein großer Konkurrent um den Titel als Erfinder der Fotografie, 1841 eine Wohnung in der Londoner Cecil Street mit der festen Absicht, sie als Studio zu nutzen und von hier aus die Stadt zu fotografieren. Außerdem bot sie nahezu identische Blickwinkel auf den Fluss, wie sie ein Jahrhundert zuvor von Canaletto gemalt wurden. Sechs von Talbots London-Bildern blieben erhalten – darunter eines, das den Bau der von Brunel erbauten Hungerford Hängebrücke über die Themse zeigt und ein weiteres der letzten Bauphase der Nelsonsäule. Keines der Bilder ist jedoch eine vertikale Komposition. Die einzig andere Ansicht Londons aus der Anfangszeit der Fotografie ist eine Daguerreotypie-Platte, die das von Wren und Hooke entworfene „The Monument to the Great Fire" von 1667 zeigt – wahrscheinlich von Antoine Claudet oder Richard Beard um 1842 aufgenommen. Es könnte die früheste „London Vertical"-Aufnahme sein.

Der Fortschritt in der neuen und unerprobten Kunst des „Festhaltens eines Schattens" wurde bereits Mitte 1840 auf innovative Weise genutzt, um das Leben und die Architektur von Städten einzufangen. Ein Beispiel hierzu ist ein halbes Dutzend sehr seltener und bemerkenswert detaillierter 140-Grad-Panoramaaufnahmen von Paris, die um 1845 auf gebogenen Daguerreotypie-Platten von dem Künstler Frédéric Martens mit einer selbst erfundenen Drehobjektivkamera aufgenommen wurden. Das gemalte Panorama als Kunstform und Spektakel war eine Erfindung, die in vielerlei Hinsicht dem Zeitgeist entsprach. Die ersten Versuche Ende des 18. Jahrhunderts legten den Grundstein zu dem, was wir heute Fotografie nennen. Gewiss verdankt Daguerre sein anfängliches Glück und seinen Ruf seiner eigenen Version (die er Diorama nannte). Aber es war London selbst, als Gastgeber und Themengeber der ersten erfolgreichen öffentlichen Präsentation des neuen Spektakels: Das von Robert Barker im Januar 1792 gezeigte Panorama am Leicester Square als „ein Blick auf die Städte LONDON und WESTMINSTER, mit den drei Brücken, die alle auf einem GEMÄLDE auf einer Fläche von 1749 Quadratfuß festgehalten und die so groß sind, dass sie in jeder Hinsicht der Realität entsprechen". Dies war so erfolgreich, dass Barker ein Jahr später die Möglichkeit hatte, die erste Panoramarotunde am Leicester Square zu errichten, was sehr schnell zu einer beliebten Form der Unterhaltung in London wurde. Dieser Erfolg wurde in europäischen Städten wie Paris bis zum Ende des 19. Jahrhunderts schnell nachgeahmt und taucht bis heute in vielen Formen als öffentliche Unterhaltung auf der ganzen Welt immer wieder auf.

Wie Martens Erfindung der Drehobjektivkamera aus dem Jahr 1845 zeigt (was eine neue technische Antwort auf die in der ersten Hälfte des 19. Jahrhunderts zu beobachtende Faszination der Öffentlichkeit für Panoramabilder war), haben die frühen Fotografen ihre malenden Kollegen mit der Entwicklung des neuen Mediums schnell imitiert und fotografische Panoramadrucke von Städten und anderen spektakulären Aussichten der natürlichen, vom Menschen geschaffenen und sozialen Welt in der Öffentlichkeit immer beliebter gemacht. Aber diese ultrabreiten Aufnahmen – ob von einer Bergkette, einer Stadt, dem Ort einer berühmten Schlacht oder einer großen Menschenmenge – waren fast immer im Querformat. Anfangs bestanden die Drucke in der Regel aus sich überlappenden Negativen, wurden aber später zunehmend mit speziellen Weitwinkel- und in einigen Fällen mit Stereokameras aufgenommen, bei denen eines der beiden Objektive entfernt wurde. Dadurch konnte mit einem zentralen Objektiv eine Halb-Panorama-Ansicht auf einer einzigen Platte aufgenommen werden. Schließlich tauchten Ende des 19. Jahrhunderts rotierende Kameras wie die Circuit-Kamera auf, die ein Bild von bis zu 360 Grad aufnehmen konnte – eine vollständige Rundumansicht. Daher assoziiert die Öffentlichkeit die Panoramafotografie nun meistens mit etwas Breitem und nicht mit etwas Aufrechtem (trotz Beispiele in der orientalischen Kunst, in der es verschiedene Formen von Panoramen im Hochformat gibt).

So scheint es bemerkenswert, dass es bis Ende der 1980er Jahre, als Horst Hamann sein großes und innovatives Projekt begann, einen der visuell markantesten Aspekte New Yorks – die charakteristische Vertikalität – zu fotografieren, nur wenige Fotografen gab (erwähnenswert ist hier Berenice Abbott mit ihrem Projekt „Changing New York" aus den 1930er Jahren), die diesen Aspekt mit aller Konsequenz und Tiefe im Verhältnis zu dem, was damals ein zunehmend dominantes Merkmal der modernen Stadt war, erforschten. Auch in Museen finden sich fast vergessene Relikte, die darauf hindeuten, dass es bereits erste Versuche zum Thema vertikale Fotografie gab. Ein oder zwei amerikanische Kamerahersteller des späten 19. und frühen 20. Jahrhunderts produzierten seltene und hoch spezialisierte großformatige „Wolkenkratzer-Kameras" aus Holz, die einem schmalen und lang gezogenen Kasten ähnelten, auf dem ein Objektiv relativ weit oben angebracht war, damit ein vertikales rechteckiges Bild (oder vertikales Panorama) ohne konvergierende Vertikalen entstehen konnte; zweifellos eine Antwort auf die Nachfrage nach einer Kamera, mit der man solche Gebäude zu Beginn der Wolkenkratzer-Ära von der Straße aus fotografieren konnte. Aber nur wenige mit einer solchen Kamera aufgenommenen Abzüge sind erhalten und dieser Aspekt der frühen Kameratechnik scheint weitgehend in Vergessenheit geraten zu sein.

Auf der Suche nach einer neuen Vision für die amerikanische Großstadt, in der Horst Hamann als junger Fotograf lebte und die bereits seit dem 19. Jahrhundert von den großen und weniger großen Fotografen endlos dokumentiert wurde, begann er, mit einer Linhof Technorama zu experimentieren – einem großen und ganz speziellen Kameratyp, der vor allem von Fotografen verwendet wurde, um breite horizontale Panoramaaufnahmen auf Rollfilm (Format 6×17 cm) mit einem Seitenverhältnis von 1:3 aufzunehmen; eine Kamera, die seit Anfang der 1980er Jahre bei Werbefotografen beliebt war, um Letterbox-Aufnahmen für die damals populären Plakatwechsler zu produzieren, aber auch bei Architekturfotografen für die Aufnahme von Gebäuden im Querformat.

Als junger Fotograf war Horst Hamann von den mit einer Technorama-Kamera aufgenommenen Bildern des deutschen Architekten und Fotografen Klaus Kinold so sehr beeindruckt, dass er schließlich eine solche Kamera für seinen eigenen Gebrauch erwarb. Er nahm die Kamera von Deutschland mit nach Amerika, konnte dort aber keine für ihn zufriedenstellenden Bilder aufnehmen und erst als er 1991 nach neuen Ansichten in der Stadt suchte, hatte er die zündende Idee: „Mir wurde plötzlich klar, dass sich in New York alles im Himmel

abspielt." Indem er die Kamera so auf die Seite drehte, dass sie hochkant stand mit einem Bildausschnitt in einem Seitenverhältnis von etwa 1:3, dachte Horst Hamann, er könne doch versuchen, auf dynamische Weise genau das einzufangen, was New York seit dem letzten Jahrhundert so unverwechselbar gemacht hat: Die Vertikalität seiner Gebäude, aus der Sicht eines normalen Bewohners oder Besuchers der Stadt. „Das allerletzte Bild, das ich auf einer Filmrolle mit der Technorama gemacht habe, war eine vertikale Komposition. Als ich es auf dem Kontaktabzug sah, dachte ich: Wow! Das funktioniert!". Von da an war "think vertical" sein Motto und sein erstes Buch mit seinen in den Jahren 1991 bis 1995 entstandenen Fotografien von New York Vertical war ein großer Erfolg.

In der Architekturfotografie brach Hamann radikal mit einigen altbewährten Konventionen, insbesondere mit der Vorgabe, dass vertikale Linien immer parallel im Bild zu halten sind, da sonst das fotografierte Gebäude verzerrt erscheint (vor allem für die Architekten als Hauptauftraggeber der Fotografen). Das ist natürlich nur eine visuelle Konvention: Wenn man auf dem Bürgersteig steht und zu einem hohen Gebäude aufschaut, dann sieht man, dass seine Seiten immer näher zusammenrücken, je höher man blickt, was nur die unkorrigierte Kamera sehen kann. Wenn wir nach oben schauen, stellt unser Gehirn lediglich die Vorstellung wieder her, dass die Seiten des Gebäudes parallel bleiben. Aufgrund der Nachfrage nach Wahrhaftigkeit in der architektonischen Bildsprache in den letzten 150 Jahren haben Kameradesigner – und in jüngster Zeit auch Software-Programmierer – geniale Möglichkeiten entwickelt, vertikale Aufnahmen zu machen und die entstehenden Bilder so zu entzerren, dass keine stürzenden Linien entstehen. Dabei bedient man sich einer geometrischen Regel, der sogenannten Scheimpflugschen Regel, die eigenartigerweise auch bei der komplexen Augenchirurgie eingesetzt wird. Technische Kameras und einige von Architekturfotografen gerne für ihre Spiegelreflexkameras verwendeten Tilt-und-Shift-Objektive bedienen sich dieser Regel bei der Gestaltung des Bildausschnittes, um durch eine Verschiebung der Linsen sowohl die Schärfeebene als auch die Objektebene anzupassen, und so die Parallelität wiederherzustellen. Bei digitalen Bildern wendet eine Software übrigens die gleiche Regel an. Fotografen benötigen in den meisten Fällen auch ein Stativ und eine Wasserwaage, da die Kamera fest positioniert sein muss, um sowohl die Schärfe- als auch die Objektivebene anhand der Scheimpflugschen Regel auf das Motiv abzustimmen. Und das schränkt die geeigneten Orte für die Fotografie ein.

Handkameras und die Scheimpflugsche Regel sind daher nicht leicht miteinander zu vereinbaren. Die meisten von Horst Hamann verwendeten Kameras lassen diese Art der Bildmanipulation nicht zu, gerade weil die Art der Bilder, die er machen will, von der Mobilität und nicht von der Statik leben. Wenn also ein von ihm fotografiertes Gebäude parallele Linien zu haben scheint, kann dies nur aus den gesuchten und gefundenen Blickwinkeln resultieren, an denen die Struktur auch wirklich so gesehen werden kann. New York war in der Tat sein Studienobjekt für diese neue Form der Fotografie und der Ort, an dem er seine neue Vision für die Stadt entwickelte: Ein Projekt, das bis zur Veröffentlichung über vier Jahre dauerte, 400 Filmrollen verschlang und 1600 Negative produzierte. Aber die Fotografie selbst ist bei solchen Projekten nur die Spitze des Eisbergs: Voran geht ein fast endloser Prozess der Standortsuche aus den buchstäblich Millionen von Möglichkeiten in den großen Metropolen wie New York (und später Paris und London). Hinzu kommen ein oft schwieriger Zugang zum gewählten Standort, das Warten auf optimale Lichtverhältnisse sowie die Auswahl des Bildausschnitts, die seiner Vorstellung einer perfekten Aufnahme entsprechen.

Für die Fotografien der Serie „London Vertical" hat sich Horst Hamann ein intensives und oft anstrengendes Arbeitspensum auferlegt, das, wie er es ausdrückt, aus „laufen, laufen, laufen" bestand, manchmal bis zu 15 Stunden am Stück für eine Fotoserie, die normalerweise jeweils bis zu vier Tage dauern kann. Die dazu gehörende sorgfältige und detaillierte Untersuchung der Architektur der Metropole – historisch, modern und zeitgenössisch – half ihm, die Aufnahmen zu machen, die seiner Vision von London in der zweiten Dekade des 21. Jahrhunderts entspricht.

In den rund dreißig Jahren zwischen dem Fotografieren für New York Vertical und „London Vertical" haben sich auch Horst Hamanns Arbeitsmittel weiterentwickelt: Die große Linhof Technorama wurde für sein nächstes Projekt Paris Vertical in den Jahren 1997 bis 2004 durch eine viel kleinere Hasselblad X-Pan 35 mm analoge Kamera ersetzt, die ebenfalls mit dem gleichen Seitenverhältnis 1:3 arbeitete.

Zehn Jahre später würde es für das im Jahr 2015 begonnene Buch über London einen weiteren technischen Fortschritt geben: Diesmal hat er für die hier gezeigten Bilder eine Digitalkamera benutzt, allerdings eine sehr spezifische und ungewöhnliche Kamera, die für die Aufnahme seiner charakteristischen Schwarz-Weiß-Bilder hoch optimiert ist.

Die Leica M Monochrom ist das Nachfolgemodell der ersten Kleinbildkamera aus dem Jahr 1925, die die „Straßenfotografie" im 20. Jahrhundert neu definierte. Diese Kamera und ihre Nachfolgemodelle sind für viele große Künstler das Medium ihrer Wahl: von Aleksandr Rodchenko, Lucia Moholy-Nagy, Henri Cartier-Bresson und Gisèle Freund bis hin zu Robert Frank, Mary Ellen Mark und Sebastião Salgado – um nur einige zu nennen. Obwohl die Monochrom praktisch die gleiche Größe wie die allererste Leica hat (und sogar die originalen Leitz-Objektive verwendet werden können), ist sie im Inneren natürlich etwas anders, da die mechanischen, für die Belichtung von 36 Bildern eines Rollfilms mit Perforationsrand erforderlichen Komponenten durch die für die digitale Aufnahme benötigte Elektronik ersetzt wurde. Das Wesen der Leica-Fotografie bleibt jedoch gleich: Es gibt einen Sucher, ein manuell fokussierbares Objektiv mit Blendenring und ein Einstellrad für die Belichtungszeiten. Der Fotograf muss einfach das Bild einfangen, das Objektiv scharf stellen und sich für die optimale Kombination von Blende und Belichtungszeit entscheiden, um sein Foto zu schießen.

Ein Vierteljahrhundert „Vertikales Denken" haben Horst Hamanns fotografische Wahrnehmungen so präzise geschliffen, dass er seine Panoramakompositionen „vorvisualisieren" kann – wie Ansel Adams es formuliert hätte. Mental komponiert er vertikal, indem er das Seitenverhältnis 1:3 vor seinem geistigen Auge sieht, noch bevor er durch den Sucher seiner Leica blickt.

Neben der künstlerischen Interpretation einer modernen Stadt wie London kann ein Fotograf wie Horst Hamann eine weitere wichtige Rolle für unser visuelles Erbe spielen. Der Fotograf ist nicht nur der Schöpfer eindrucksvoller Bilder, sondern auch ein privilegierter Chronist eines tief greifenden Wandels im urbanen Gefüge. Wie Horst Hamann selbst betont und in seinen Arbeiten zu New York, Paris und jetzt London so eindrucksvoll unter Beweis gestellt hat, wird die Architektur der Stadt als visuelles Umfeld zunehmend von der vertikalen Dimension dominiert. Und auch wir als Bewohner oder Besucher der Stadt sind dadurch gezwungen, unsere visuellen Vorstellungen anzupassen.

Die Fotografie spielt nun seit etwa 200 Jahren beim Verständnis der visuellen, kulturellen und sozialen Auswirkungen von langfristigen Veränderungen im Wesen, der Funktion und der Form der Stadt eine wichtige Rolle, und zwar auf eine weitaus aussagekräftigere Art und Weise als jede andere Kunst. Diese Veränderungen sind nur allzu offensichtlich, wenn man sich die Zeit nimmt, um zum Beispiel die Fotografien von „London Vertical" mit denen in einer kürzlich im English Heritage Verlag erschienenen Publikation „Panoramas of Lost London" zu vergleichen. Letztere dokumentiert die Gebäude und die Silhouette der Stadt, die in London aus verschiedenen Gründen, vor allem aber durch Feuer, Krieg, Verfall und Stadterneuerung in den Jahren 1870–1945, zerstört wurden. Obwohl es sich dabei nicht um wirkliche Panoramafotografien handelt, zeigen die überwiegend aus den Archiven des London County Council stammenden und aus sehr großformatigen Negativen und Druckgrafiken heraus vergrößerten Detailaufnahmen eine Metropole ab 1880, in der sich die vertikal dominierenden Gebäude – vor allem Kirchen, Kathedralen und Denkmäler wie die Nelsonsäule oder „The Monument to the Great Fire" selbst – in ihrer ganzen Pracht zeigen und sich von der dominanten Masse beeindruckender, aber im Wesentlichen horizontaler Gebäude, die London im späten 19. und der ersten Hälfte des 20. Jahrhunderts prägen, abheben.

Hamanns neueste Fotografien von London dokumentieren natürlich einige jener bekannten vertikalen Gebäude, die ein Londoner aus dem Jahr 1918 auch noch ein Jahrhundert später erkennen würde. Lässt man jedoch jene Bilder außer Betracht, die dasselbe Gebäude mehr als einmal als Teil einer Komposition enthalten, bleiben nur eine Handvoll Gebäude aus dem 17. bis 19. Jahrhundert als charakteristische Merkmale des zeitgenössischen Londoner Stadtbildes übrig. Und selbst diese werden in vielen Fällen von weitaus jüngeren Bauten aus dem 21. Jahrhundert überschattet. Nur wenige dieser Neubauten sind architektonisch und planungsrechtlich unumstritten. Viele werden von der Öffentlichkeit mit sozialen, politischen und wirtschaftlichen Veränderungen in Verbindung gebracht, die weithin als spaltend und ungerecht erachtet werden. Ein

besonderes Beispiel ist der Sky Garden in der Fenchurch Street, das so genannte „Walkie-Talkie", dessen breite Form an der Spitze die Tatsache widerspiegelt, dass in London die gezahlten Mieten umso teurer sind, je höher die Flächen liegen. Die Zeitung „The Guardian" kommentierte das wie folgt: „Als buchstäbliches Zeichen der Gier der Entwickler liefert es den schmerzhaften Beweis, dass die Form nicht der Funktion, sondern dem Geld folgt. Das Gebäude ist ein Irrtum des Stadtplanungssystems, das völlig isoliert, wie ein aus dem Klassenzimmer verbannter Rädelsführer, außerhalb des City-Clusters liegt und mit seiner unwillkommenen Masse fast alle möglichen Blickwinkel der Skyline verzerrt."

Ganz gleich wie man die „Vertikalisierung" Londons in den letzten Jahrzehnten betrachtet, ist es vielleicht hilfreich, das Stadtgebiet von London mit Paris zu vergleichen. Denn trotz der unzähligen und oft trostlosen Hochhäuser in den Banlieues außerhalb der Périphérique, durfte nur ein einziger Wolkenkratzer das von Charles Marville (einem weiteren Vorgänger von Horst Hamann) auf dem Höhepunkt städtebaulichen Umgestaltung ab 1860 durch Haussmann so eindringlich eingefangene Pariser Stadtbild zerstören: der Tour Montparnasse. Ein Bauwerk, das so umstritten und unbeliebt war, dass zwei Jahre nach seiner Fertigstellung im Jahr 1973 Neubauten mit mehr als sieben Stockwerken im Stadtzentrum verboten wurden. Einige mögen argumentieren, dass es eine Schande ist, dass der Bürgermeister von London nie eine ähnliche Entscheidung getroffen hat.

Trotz der zahlreichen Kontroversen über die Entwicklung hoher Gebäude in London ab 1960 ist es erstaunlich, dass es nur sehr wenige renommierte Fotobücher von führenden Fotografen über diese Stadt gibt, die sich hauptsächlich auf ihre gebaute Form konzentrieren. Selbst Klassiker des Fotobuch-Genres, die sich mit London beschäftigen und von richtungsweisenden Fotografen gemacht wurden, wie zum Beispiel „Charmes de Londres" von Izis mit einem Text von Jacques Prévert (Guilde du Livre, 1952: Ebenfalls in englischer Sprache erschienen), sind vergleichsweise rar und konzentrieren sich selten auf die gebaute Umwelt, vor allem im Vergleich zu denen in Paris und New York, und meines Wissens gab es von niemandem bisher vertikale Panoramafotos.

Neben den Werken von Marville, die zu seinen Lebzeiten nie in Buchform veröffentlicht wurden, ist vielleicht ein anderes Buch mit Panoramafotografien von Josef Sudek, eine sehr seltene und begehrte Fotogravurpublikation über Prag, „Praha panoramaticka" aus dem Jahr 1956 mit den Werken von Horst Hamann vergleichbar. Sie bestehen hauptsächlich aus horizontalen Panoramabildern, enthalten aber auch einige vertikale Aufnahmen. Es überrascht vielleicht nicht, dass das Werk des Prager Meisters von Horst Hamann sehr bewundert wird. Beide haben in ihren Bildern ein ähnliches Gespür für das Gleichgewicht von Licht, Raum und Form. Ich wage die Prognose, dass die Qualität der Visionen und Einzigartigkeit seiner Fotografien „London Vertical" zu einem Buch machen werden, das in den kommenden Jahren genauso begehrt sein wird wie das des berühmten tschechischen Vorgängers von Horst Hamann.

Horst Hamann was born in Mannheim in 1958 and has been taking photographs since age eleven. He has spent half of his life in New York City and the State of Maine. He is often referred to as the "inventor" of vertical photography. The "New York Times" has named him a "genius of composition". The Museum of the City of New York has honoured him as the first German photographer with a six-month solo exhibition. Horst Hamann is the author of more than 45 books. His "verticals" are milestones in the world of photography. The book "New York Vertical" became a worldwide best seller. In 2015 he received the German Photobook Award for his book "Absolute NY". In 2022 Hamann opened the Gallery NY in his hometown Mannheim.

Michael Hoppen has been involved in photography in one form or another for over 40 years. Having attained a 1st class BA honors in photography film and television in 1980 at the LCC, and then a year at the Royal College of Art in London. Michael then ran his own studio as a commercial and art photographer, which he closed in 1991. The Michael Hoppen Gallery opened in 1992 and then Shine Gallery opened in 2000. The Michael Hoppen Gallery has also exhibited at art fairs in New York, Mexico, Hong Kong, Basel, Amsterdam, Tokyo and Paris. The gallery has worked with many of the great names and estates in photography. The Michael Hoppen Gallery and Michael Hoppen Contemporary are totally dedicated to the exhibition and publishing of photography and the gallery is dedicated to a high degree of excellence to promote the gallery's core values and shows in the appreciation of all photographic disciplines.

Roger Ridsdill Smith is Head of the Structural Engineering team at Foster + Partners. He graduated from the University of Cambridge and began his professional career in Paris. In 1994, he joined Ove Arup and Partners in London, where his projects included the London Millennium Bridge, and became a director of the firm in 2003. He joined Foster + Partners in 2011 to start the Structural Engineering team. Current projects include the new Airport and Transport Hub for Warsaw, Poland, the Ellison Institute for Transformative Medicine in Oxford, UK, and the Lusail Towers in Doha, Qatar. The team designed the competition winning structural solutions for the new towers at 425 Park Avenue and 270 Park Avenue, the JP Morgan headquarters, both in New York. Roger is an Honorary Senior Lecturer at Imperial College. He won the Royal Academy of Engineering Silver medal in 2010, and the International Association for Bridge and Structural Engineering Milne Medal in 2017.

Peter Hamilton (1947–2022), a photo historian, author and exhibition curator. After a few years working in photography studios as a youth he attended university and became an academic sociologist. From the late 1980s his research led him to work with the French photographers Robert Doisneau (1912–1994) and Willy Ronis (1910–2009), and the British photographer James Ravilious (1939–1999) on major retrospective exhibitions of their photographs. He has also curated thematic exhibitions on portrait and celebrity photography, the history of the panoramic photograph, French humanist photography, and the centenary of Leica photography for leading public galleries in the UK, Europe and North America. His books have won several prizes including the Kraszna-Krausz Award.

Horst Hamann wurde 1958 in Mannheim geboren und fotografiert seit seinem elften Lebensjahr. Die Hälfte seines Lebens hat er in New York City und im Bundesstaat Maine verbracht. Er wird oft als der „Erfinder" der vertikalen Fotografie bezeichnet. Die „New York Times" nannte ihn ein „Genie der Komposition". Das Museum of the City of New York hat ihn als ersten deutschen Fotografen mit einer sechsmonatigen Einzelausstellung geehrt. Horst Hamann ist der Autor von mehr als 45 Büchern. Seine „Verticals" sind Meilensteine in der Welt der Fotografie. Das Buch „New York Vertical" wurde ein weltweiter Bestseller. 2015 erhielt er den Deutschen Fotobuchpreis für seinen Bildband „Absolute NY". Im Jahr 2022 eröffnete Hamann die Galerie NY in seiner Heimatstadt Mannheim.

Michael Hoppen beschäftigt sich seit über 40 Jahren in der einen oder anderen Form mit Fotografie. Er erwarb 1980 am LCC einen Bachelor of Arts 1. Klasse in Fotografie, Film und Fernsehen und besuchte anschließend ein Jahr lang das Royal College of Art in London. Danach führte Michael Hoppen sein eigenes Studio als Werbe- und Kunstfotograf, das er 1991 schloss. Die Michael Hoppen Gallery wurde 1992 eröffnet und die Shine Gallery im Jahr 2000. Die Michael Hoppen Gallery hat auch auf Kunstmessen in New York, Mexiko, Hongkong, Basel, Amsterdam, Tokio und Paris ausgestellt. Die Galerie hat mit vielen der großen Namen der Fotografie zusammengearbeitet und bedeutende Nachlässe betreut. Die Michael Hoppen Gallery und Michael Hoppen Contemporary widmen sich ganz der Ausstellung und Veröffentlichung von exzellenter Fotografie.

Roger Ridsdill Smith ist Leiter des Teams für Hochbau bei Foster + Partners. Er schloss sein Studium an der Universität Cambridge ab und begann seine berufliche Laufbahn in Paris. Im Jahr 1994 kam er zu Ove Arup and Partners in London, wo er unter anderem an der Londoner Millennium Bridge mitwirkte, und wurde 2003 Direktor des Unternehmens. Seit 2011 ist er bei Foster + Partners tätig und leitet das Team für Hochbau. Zu den aktuellen Projekten gehören der neue Flughafen und der Verkehrsknotenpunkt in Warschau, Polen, das Ellison Institute for Transformative Medicine in Oxford, Großbritannien, und die Lusail Towers in Doha, Katar. Das Team entwarf die preisgekrönten Konstruktionslösungen für die neuen Türme an der 425 Park Avenue und 270 Park Avenue, dem Hauptsitz von JP Morgan, beide in New York. Roger Ridsdill Smith ist Honorary Senior Lecturer am Imperial College. Er wurde 2010 mit der Silbermedaille der Royal Academy of Engineering und 2017 mit der Milne-Medaille der International Association for Bridge and Structural Engineering ausgezeichnet.

Peter Hamilton (1947–2022), Fotohistoriker, Autor und Ausstellungskurator. Nachdem er in seiner Jugend einige Jahre in Fotostudios gearbeitet hatte, besuchte er die Universität und wurde Soziologe. Seit den späten 1980er Jahren arbeitete er mit den französischen Fotografen Robert Doisneau (1912–1994) und Willy Ronis (1910–2009) sowie dem britischen Fotografen James Ravilious (1939–1999) an großen retrospektiven Ausstellungen ihrer Fotografien. Darüber hinaus hat er für führende öffentliche Galerien in Großbritannien, Europa und Nordamerika thematische Ausstellungen über Porträt- und Prominentenfotografie, die Geschichte der Panoramafotografie, die französische humanistische Fotografie und das hundertjährige Bestehen der Leica-Fotografie kuratiert. Seine Bücher wurden mit mehreren Preisen ausgezeichnet, darunter dem Kraszna-Krausz Award.

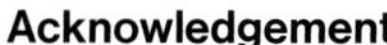

Acknowledgement

Moritz von der Linden

Roger Ridsdill Smith
Michael Hoppen
Peter Hamilton

Tilo Kaiser

Marie Preaud, Mateo and Paolo Hamann

Narinder Sagoo, Jinita Batavia, Gerda and Jörg Siebert, Andrea Patella, Bernhard und Sebastian Wipfler, Wolfgang Roth, Lou Proud, Oliver Obert, Sophie Kraft, David Kurz, Sebastian teNeues, Stefanie Penck, Nele Jansen, Stephanie Rebel, Roman Korn, Werner Rehberger, Tanja Sturm, Tabea Schorndorf, Sophie Hackford, Henny Acloque, Hope Powell, Winni Rothermel, Adam Schatz, Eli Morgan-Gesner, Janina Mock, René Winklbauer, Anna Sparham, David Ortiz, Dr. Andreas Kaufmann, Christian Duve, Peter Utsch, Sophie Nguyen, Veronique Nguyen, Cécile zu Hohenlohe, Liz and Max Haarala Hamilton, Tim Pullmann, Geraldine Pfeffer, Katy Harris, Elisabet Barone, Melissa Land, Micaela Buchanan, Mrinal Rammohan, Horst und Helen Hadergasser, Julian Zimmermann, Katy Barron, Clemency Cooke, Daniela Franz, Heinrich Gröger, Johannes Hamann, Udo van Kampen, Gabi Graze, Paul Packg, Paul Beiboer, Christel Ferino, Achim Judt, Edyta Pokrywka, Flossy Belm, Jean-Jaques Viau, Pete Littlewood, Eleonora Duddy

Lord Normann Foster for the inspiration

Thanks to Leica Camera AG Wetzlar for their generous support especially Karin Rehn-Kaufmann.

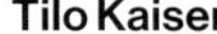